*Growing
a Reader
from Birth*

W. W. Norton & Company

NEW YORK | LONDON

Growing
a Reader
from Birth

YOUR CHILD'S PATH FROM

LANGUAGE TO LITERACY

Diane McGuinness, Ph.D.

For information about permission to reproduce selections
from this book, write to Permissions, W. W. Norton &
Company, Inc., 500 Fifth Avenue, New York, NY 10110

Manufacturing by The Courier Companies, Inc.
Book design by Barbara M. Bachman
Production manager: Amanda Morrison

Library of Congress Cataloging-in-Publication Data
McGuinness, Diane.
Growing a reader from birth : your child's path from language
to literacy / Diane McGuinness.— 1st ed.
p. cm.
Includes bibliographical references and index.
ISBN 0-393-05802-6 (hardcover)
1. Children—Language. 2. Language arts (Early childhood).
3. Reading (Early childhood). I. Title.
LB1139.L3M3345 2004
372.4—dc22

2003018131

W. W. Norton & Company, Inc.
500 Fifth Avenue, New York, N.Y. 10110
www.wwnorton.com

W. W. Norton & Company Ltd.
Castle House, 75/76 Wells Street, London W1T 3QT

1 2 3 4 5 6 7 8 9 0

Contents

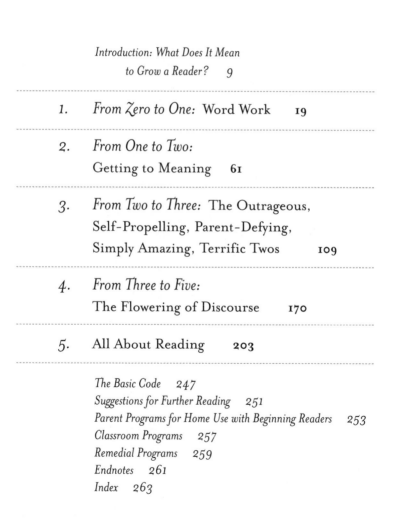

*Growing
a Reader
from Birth*

What Does It Mean to Grow a Reader?

T HE SKILLS THAT PRODUCE AN EXPERT READER ARE exactly the same skills that make an expert listener. These are the skills that allow us to *comprehend language* in all its facets and nuances. Being a good reader is *not*, as most people believe, simply the ability to decode isolated words. Decoding is certainly essential, but it is a relatively minor part of reading skill. In countries with a straightforward alphabet writing system, where each sound is represented by only one symbol, learning to 'crack the code' takes about twelve weeks for all children. The English alphabet code is highly 'opaque,' with multiple spellings for the same sound, and multiple ways to decode the same letter. Because of this, many children have unnecessary difficulties learning how to decode, and this has diverted everyone's attention from what matters most. A child who has an impoverished vocabulary, poor syntactic and semantic skills, and who is unable to make inferences, keep track of sequence, and relate pieces of information, won't understand what he reads any better than he understands what he hears.

All the evidence shows that the major predictor of becoming

a good reader is the development of good language skills during the early years of life. People can learn to decode at any age, but language skills *cannot* be taught at any age. They unfold in an intimate verbal dance between a child and his parents, and mom and dad's input is critical every step of the way. Children who are deprived of normal verbal interaction with a parent or care-taker are seriously compromised in language development, and may never recover if the deprivation is too prolonged.

The Parents' Role in the Language Dance

Over the past decade, we have learned more about language development and the parents' role in this development than in all previous decades combined. There is a biological blueprint that sets out the developmental milestones children pass through as they progress from recognizing words (auditory patterns), to understanding referential meaning (vocal noises stand for peo-ple, things, and actions), to early speech production (babbling), to that magic moment when baby says his first word and means what he says. For the average child, these accomplishments fall into place during the first year of life, give or take a few months. More complex language functions follow over the next two years.

However, the 'average' child is a statistical average, and we know that real children vary enormously in age when these milestones appear. Some children have no spoken language until eighteen months or later. Scientists are trying to determine how much these individual differences are due to innate fac-tors, such as auditory processing abilities (the ability to analyze speech patterns), speech-motor development (the ability to mimic what someone says), and specific language functions (the ability to link speech patterns to meaning), or to environmental factors (parents' input), or to the relationship between them. While the biological basis for language is not in dispute, the human race doesn't speak in some generic Esperanto. We don't have a one-size-fits-all, species-specific template for vocal patterns like birds do. Whatever the biological blueprint might be, it isn't a blueprint for a *specific* language. Any human group that has been isolated by time, space, or circumstance, will develop a unique language with novel patterns of vocal noises to stand for words, and different solutions for marking grammatical structure. A child can't rely on his biological endowment to learn a language. He must hear it being spoken. Without parents' verbal outpourings and exchanges, language development can't proceed normally, and may even shut down altogether. As to when this critical moment arrives, no one knows for sure.

The 'universal language production machine' is present in every one of us. But language isn't a product of an assembly line, like Ford Mustang carburetors. Each person's machine is ever so slightly different, and this difference is inherited. A child's verbal IQ (primarily measured by vocabulary size) comes to resemble his biological parents' verbal IQ more and more during childhood—*even if parents and child have never met.* Studies on thousands of twins and adopted children show that by the mid to late teens, about 50 percent of a child's verbal skill can be attributed to his genes (that is, highly correlated to his *biological* parents' verbal ability). Most of the other 50 percent is attributable to *shared environment.* For a young child, shared environment refers largely to what the child is exposed to in the home. This means that parents not only pass on their genes, but they can write on these genes as well, depending on how they interact vocally and emotionally with their child.

We now have a good sense of what parents are able to accomplish in this shared environment. The most exciting aspect of this work is that knowledge *really* is power. Parents can have a positive impact on their child's language and communication skills in quite specific ways. And knowing this makes it easy for parents to expand on what they're doing right, or to copy what other parents are doing right. We know a lot about what's harmful or counterproductive as well, making it possible for parents to curtail what they're doing wrong. A major goal of this book is to describe and illuminate what young children need from us at a given moment in time, and to show parents how to maximize positive verbal and social interactions with their child from birth to age five.

Language Written Down

Since the dawn of the human race, the major mode of communication has been spoken language. Spoken language exists in the ever present *now*, and unless someone memorizes the speaker's words verbatim, it can't transcend time and space. Five thousand years ago, the invention of writing changed all that. Suddenly, it became possible for conversations, messages, edicts, speeches, histories, myths, legends, court proceedings, battle plans, and poetry to be recorded in a permanent form.

A writing system is a code, or cipher, in which abstract symbols are assigned to sounds in speech. The reader decodes the symbols to understand the original message. Because this invention was so remarkable—so novel and so complex that schools had to be set up to teach it—most people identify reading with 'reading mechanics,' the ability to master the code. They forget that the reader never abandons his role as listener. His job is still to work out what the speaker (now writer) meant to say. In a way, one can think of print as a kind of filter or veil through which a speaker is trying to communicate to his listeners.

In ordinary conversations, the most important role the listener undertakes is a sincere effort to *comprehend* what the speaker intended to say. This role doesn't change just because the speaker's message is written down. In fact, the reader has to work harder because helpful cues are missing. Absent are the speaker's tone of voice, body language, and facial expressions. There are no fillers or pauses to give the listener cues about intentions and truthfulness, or time to sift his thoughts. Printed text has little or no redundancy, no unnecessary words. Characters in novels never speak in anything remotely resembling natural speech, which sounds more like this:

Well, um, um, yeah, you could say that. Um, I guess you could say that. Let me put it this way—um, um, she didn't, I mean, we didn't. Well, here's a better example.

Missing too is the background knowledge that the speaker and listener share. A reader gazing at a stark white page covered with little abstract squiggles, has to make *sense* of them, not merely by turning the sequences into words, but by turning words into *meaning*.

So while the common definition of reading as the 'ability to decode a set of symbols into speech' is technically accurate, it only scratches the surface of what a reader must be able to do. Readers need to go well beyond letters, speech sounds, and words; they must be able to access *meaning* and *imagery* to gain a full understanding of what the written symbols represent.

There are three basic skills or aptitudes a child needs to become a good reader and speller, and these abilities don't necessarily go together. The ability to decode (translating symbols into speech sounds) is the gateway to reading, because without it there is no access to the printed page. Encoding (turning speech sounds into symbols) is the gateway to *written* expression. To read, spell, and write means to engage auditory, visual, and fine-motor skills. Children must be able to tell the various letter shapes apart and remember them. They must be able to hear the individual speech sounds the letters stand for and learn to match letters and sounds correctly 100 percent of the time. The memory skill needed for memorizing abstract shapes and sounds, and for remembering which sound goes with which shape develops rather late, at around age four.

The second skill is the ability to read fluently. A reader should not only be able to decode print accurately, she should also be quick about it. If decoding proceeds too slowly, the reader won't understand what she reads. Imagine how difficult it would be to read this book if there was only one word on each page. Reading speed is already slow at the best of times. People can speak at an astonishing two hundred to three hundred words per minute, an optimum rate for the brain to extract meaning from spoken language. The expert college reader reads at about the same speed. The average second grader reads eighty words per minute. When reading speed falls below this level, comprehension is difficult if not impossible.

Reading speed isn't an isolated skill. It's a function of decoding accuracy, text difficulty, and general language ability. Good readers are able to predict or anticipate which words are likely to come next in the sentence, and this dramatically increases reading speed. A good reader is exactly like a good listener. This is someone who anticipates the words the speaker is *likely* to say based on her knowledge of grammar, language use (colloquialisms), and familiarity with the topic. Listeners are always well ahead of the game. This is why puns, word play, and jokes make us laugh. They breach our expectations of what we thought the speaker was *about to say* or should have said.

A child who merely decodes the symbols may get the words right, but unless those words are in his vocabulary, they have nowhere to go. They're registered by the brain as 'not at home,' or 'no address.' They float around in brain space, then fade from memory, faint echoes that die away. A good reader needs a rich vocabulary and facility with the grammatical structure of his language.

It will come as a surprise to many readers that children can be able to decode letter symbols and identify words with great accuracy, yet not be able to understand what they read. The most extraordinary account comes from a study done in Italy on children with Down's syndrome. These children were profoundly mentally retarded, with IQs in the 40s (100 is average). Despite this, they spoke in sentences. They could carry on 'conversations,' waiting their turn to speak and making eye contact, though they barely understood what was said to them, and their responses often didn't make sense. Yet every one of these children could read. That is, they could *decode*. They scored in the age range of a normal eight-year-old on a difficult reading test, accurately decoding complex multisyllable words like *sbagliari* and *funebre*. But when they were asked about what they read, they didn't know the topic, the names of the characters, the events in the story, or anything else. There are scores of documented cases of children who read fluently and accurately but don't comprehend what they read.

These facts tell us something very important about the link between language and reading. Learning the letters of the alphabet and which one(s) matches which speech sound, though essential, is a relatively minor part of the reading process. *Understanding* what is read is far more important. Studies on children's reading comprehension show that the most powerful predictor of reading comprehension is not decoding accuracy or reading speed, but *listening comprehension*, the ability to understand what someone says. You can predict performance on a reading comprehension test with about 50 percent accuracy from a measure of listening comprehension, while decoding skill (reading isolated words) predicts reading comprehension by only 10 percent. The two skills in combination are more powerful than either one alone, and predict reading comprehension with 70 percent accuracy. In the world of statistics, this is about as good as it gets.[*]

Listening comprehension and learning a writing system need different kinds of input and different types of training, and they operate on different clocks. If the foundation for growing a reader is good language skills, most critically a good vocabulary, knowledge of grammatical structure, and verbal memory, how does this knowledge come about? How is it that when six-year-old Jessica reads "The little bunnies huddled in the dense grass near their burrow," she conjures up a vivid image of brown bunnies sitting snuggled together in medium-height, closely knit, green grass near a hole leading to their burrow? Jessica can even imagine the burrow underneath, snug and dry. Yet six-year-old Jason, who scores just as high as Jessica on tests of reading accuracy and fluency, can only imagine 'bunnies' and 'grass.' Jason has never heard of a burrow. He doesn't know that rabbits live in them. He has never heard the words 'huddle' or 'dense' before. His brain 'knows' that *huddle* is a verb because of where it comes in the sentence. In English, verbs follow the subject. We don't say "huddle the bunnies" or "the huddle bunnies." He knows this implicitly, not consciously, just as his brain 'knows' that *dense* has something to do with the grass. In English, adjec-

---

[*] For readers familiar with statistics, the correlation between listening comprehension and reading comprehension is $r = .70$, between decoding and reading comprehension $r = .30$, and for both together $r = .84$.

tives precede the nouns they qualify. We don't say "the grass dense."

From Jason's perspective, while he reads correctly: "The little bunnies huddled in the dense grass near their burrow," he understands only this: "The little bunnies—in the—grass near their—" He has some vague ideas that his brain has shared with him, like the bunnies are doing something called 'huddle'; the grass isn't just grass because it is something called 'dense'; and the bunnies are sitting near something called a 'burrow'—perhaps a 'bunny mother'? Even if there were a picture, it wouldn't give Jason many more clues than his own brain did.

What makes Jessica different from Jason is YOU, the parent. Genes may play a role in language development, grammatical accuracy, vocabulary, and memory, but genes are far from being the whole story. What matters most is *how* and *how much* mothers and fathers speak and read to their children *from day one*. As parents, we have a biological program to help us carry out this task. But we can be more effective when we're aware of what we're doing and why. It helps enormously to know what children need from us at a particular time in their development. Children are never passive about communication and language. They begin to process speech in the womb. Babies do their best to engage us in the games and activities that will eventually make them sophisticated users of a language, the key to becoming an expert reader. Your own child can be your best teacher if you tune in. This book is about helping you enhance your child's journey from babbling to decoding the written word.

About This Book

This book is set out in chronological order from just before birth to age five. Each chapter describes the latest research on language and cognitive development and provides ways for parents to engage their child in learning appropriate skills. The chronological order makes it convenient for you to find information about your child more easily, and to focus on those skills your child is able to perform. Remember that there is nothing magical about a particular age. A child's first word can appear as early as ten months and as late as two years, and this is perfectly normal.

You should also be aware that infants and young children understand a lot more than they can express. In technical jargon, *language perception precedes language production.* Not only do babies understand a lot more than you might imagine, they are also mentally working out some of the finer implications. They have a much harder time trying to put their ideas and thoughts into words. Because so much of language development is hidden, you should read this book from the beginning. You'll find out what your child has been doing and how far she has progressed along the way. When you understand this progression, you'll be better equipped to anticipate what she will be doing next.

Most of this book is directed to the development of natural language and language comprehension. Language comprehension is not just about what the words mean. It is about every mental process that helps us interpret the world. It's about knowledge, about understanding time, sequence, and causality, about empathy, logic, and inference. Our discussion draws on a rich resource, a wealth of fascinating information about how parents can help their children develop sophisticated language and thinking skills, and it concludes with practical advice on reading instruction. The good news is that we know *exactly* what children need to be taught to insure that every child will learn to read.

Word Work

Listening in the Womb

HEARING, ALONG WITH TOUCH, ARE THE FIRST SENSES to begin developing during gestation. By the third trimester (six to nine months) all the connections from the ear through the five relay points to the higher brain cortex are in place. Each neural relay has grown a fatty sheath that makes rapid transmission possible from the sensory organs of the ear almost to the auditory cortex. Although hearing starts developing early, the higher brain organization takes a long time to complete. This differs from vision, which starts later and is completed early.

The changes in the nervous system parallel the baby's experience. At around the sixth month, the baby's peaceful inner sanctum starts to become a buzzing tapestry of sounds. There is the whooshing of blood and fluids, the steady beat of the mother's heart, and loud sounds from the external world. Above and beyond this, is the mother's voice, louder in the womb than it is for people listening outside. The mother's voice is carried to the womb internally by her bones, which resonate with the sounds. Like most people, you might imagine that the baby's auditory world is a blooming, buzzing, confusion, a cacophony where nothing can be heard with distinctness or clarity.

This belief was shattered in 1986 when an amazing study appeared in *Science*. A. J. De Caspar and H. J. Spence discovered that newborns could recognize a Dr. Seuss story that they had been listening to in the womb. The experiment went like this: For the last six weeks of pregnancy, mothers read *The Cat in the Hat* two times each day. They read in a normal voice with lots of animated expression as if they were reading to a four-year-old. Just after the babies were born, they were tested on their preference for mom's rendition of either *The Cat in the Hat* or *The King, the Mice, and the Cheese*, a story they had never heard. The babies' interest was measured by the amount of sucking they did on a dummy nipple. The babies sucked faster and longer for *The Cat in the Hat*.

Since that time a flood of research studies has revealed what unborn babies can do. For the most part, these remarkable feats begin to appear sometime around the sixth month of pregnancy. Many studies took advantage of the new technology developed for fetal heart rate monitoring. The unborn babies' heart rates were monitored to see if changes would occur in response to different auditory signals. When we pay attention to something, our heart rate slows noticeably. In part this is caused by a sharp reduction in movement. Heart rate goes up when you move and down when you don't. It's hard to pay attention when you're fidgeting or in motion. Unborn babies are no exception: Their heart rates slow when they hear something that interests them; they stop moving to listen, the same way we do.

Using this technique to measure interest or attention, different scientists working in different countries made the following discoveries. First, unborn babies are interested in hearing mom talk. Mothers-to-be were asked to say, "Hello, baby, how are you today?" and repeat this phrase several times. After hearing this one or two times, the baby's heart slowed dramatically. And it did so right on cue each time mother said this phrase. The heart rate response didn't occur during silence or when she whispered the same phrase repeatedly. In a variation of the original study on Dr. Seuss, mothers were asked to say a simple rhyme to their unborn child every day for the last four weeks of pregnancy (thirty-three to thirty-seven weeks). Babies' heart rate responses slowed more for the familiar nursery rhyme than for one they had never heard before.

Second, unborn babies learn to recognize patterns of sounds coming from outside the womb, especially music. In a study in Ireland, some pregnant moms listened to a particular soap opera every day and some did not. When the unborn babies whose moms had listened to the soap opera heard the theme song, their heart rates went down. Babies who had never heard the theme song had no reaction. In a different study, heart rate patterns showed that unborn babies noticed the difference between rock music and classical music played at the same volume.

Finally, unborn babies are sensitive to different syllable patterns in the womb. In a famous French study, babies heard the word *baby* repeated over and over again from a speaker pressed to the mother's tummy. After hearing *baby* a few times, the babies' heart rate slowed each time the word was repeated. Eventually, the heart rate response stopped. Baby was bored with *baby*. At this point, the syllables were reversed: *beebay*. Immediately, heart rate slowed once more: The baby noticed the difference between *baby* and *beebay*.

Taken together, these studies illustrate a consistent pattern. Babies in utero may or may not pay attention to something they hear for the first time, but if it is clear enough, loud enough, and repeats for a while, it will capture their attention, especially if it's mother's voice. Once captured, unless what is heard is extremely short, repetitive, and boring, the baby will remain interested in this now familiar pattern of sounds. Of course, unborn babies don't recognize words as such. They learn mom's patterns of speech, its pitch and rhythm. This also explains their ability to recognize or prefer different kinds of music. They respond to the overall sound quality and the rhythm pattern, not to a specific melody or harmonic structure.

The French research shows that unborn babies have a special talent for hearing patterns of sounds in words or syllables. This is quite extraordinary, because it means babies come into the world primed to process and analyze the sound structure (or phonological structure) of a language, and are all set to go at day one.

Feats of the Newborn

It's Important How You Say What You Say

YOUR NEW INFANT IS HERE. She is a seven-pound, eight-ounce bundle with an amazing brain that has evolved for the purpose of finding out about you and her world. She has been consoled by the sound of your voice for at least three months. Now she gets to meet you. She may seem helpless and a little bit dozy, but she is a budding Einstein compared to what some 'experts' believe, and even a lot smarter than moms (who have more sense) believe.

She knows how to behave in ways that will produce just the right responses from you, and *you* know (but didn't know you knew) just the right thing to do back. If this is your first child, you will find yourself talking and behaving in a way you never dreamed possible. There is something about that little, helpless figure, with those unblinking eyes that stare quizzically into your own, that makes you alter your voice and manner. You find yourself saying:

Helllooo liiiituull keeeooteeee piiiiiie. Mommmeeeez littuuull Jehnnnneeee. Helllooo baaaaaybee Jehnnnneeee, liiiitttulll Jehnnnneeee. Helllooo baaaaaybee.

What has come over you? And not only you, but dad, your parents, the next-door neighbor, and even grumpy Uncle George who swears he won't talk like that, but he does. This pattern of speech, reserved exclusively for tiny babies, is called Motherese. It is a kind of biological CD that babies know how to turn on and extract from us with that stare and their cute little round, red cheeks.

Scientists have devoted thousands of hours to investigating Motherese. What exactly is it? Does it have anything to do with how the baby hears? Does it have anything to do with helping the baby learn language? Does it make the baby feel good? It turns out that Motherese, *but not baby talk* (is my itsy-bitsy babykins happy?) is just about perfect for baby in every respect.

Motherese is obviously very different from conversational speech. It is high-pitched, about one octave higher than normal speech. It is excessively modulated so that the pitch changes across a very wide range (something I tried to illustrate in the example above). It is excessively slowed down, and all the sounds are stretched, particularly the vowels. Phrases are short and often repeated. The vocabulary is simple but not artificial, and the words are enunciated clearly. The stress patterns in words are emphasized. Motherese has its greatest impact when delivered in a loud animated voice about one foot from baby's face.

I don't have to tell you to do it; you will be doing it. But it is interesting to know why. Babies have poor hearing in the sense that they need to hear things much louder than adults do. They also have a limited range of pitches that they are sensitive to, so raising the pitch of your voice fits what they hear best. Despite these limitations, they are amazingly sensitive to the sounds in words, especially consonant-vowel combinations, so slowing words down and stretching out each vowel helps them notice these patterns more easily.

Baby's First Word

AS BABIES BEGIN the long road to becoming master wordsmiths, the hardest thing they have to do is find out where the words stop and start in a stream of speech. When we speak, our words don't have neat little spaces between them like words on a page. Everything runs together: "Jimcouldyoufeedthebaby whileImakedinner?" Somehow, baby has to figure out where a word is in this auditory mélange.

What do you suppose little Jenny is hearing when you say:

Hellloooo liiiituull keeooteeee piiiiiiie. Mommmeeeez littuuull Jehnnnneeee. Helllooo baaaaybee Jehnnnneeee, liiiitttulll Jehnnnneeee. Helllooo baaaaaybee.

Through some clever tricks, scientists have been able to let babies show us what they know. We have learned, for example, that babies will hear all these sounds pretty much the same as you say them, except, of course, it won't make any sense. It will take a while to get the sounds sorted and filed. But by the age of four and a half months, careful testing shows that Jenny will recognize (remember) only one word out of everything you and the rest of the family have said to her up to that point, and that is: *Jenny.*

Your child's name is her first word, at least in her thoughts. Even though you say *mommy* and *daddy* a lot of the time, she won't recognize these words until around six or seven months. Of course Jenny has heard her name a lot, too, more than any other word. And it carries a wallop of meaning, because it is meant only for her. Does this mean that you can train Jenny's vocabulary by sheer repetition?

mommy mommy mommy mommy mommy
mommy mommy mommy mommy

Well yes, it does, if you want to bother with this. This is what the study on the unborn French babies showed. But it won't help Jenny learn to talk or to use all those special skills of hers to find words in context and learn to communicate. Jenny needs a lot more. She needs hours and hours of conversation with you to exercise each one of her skills. Chanting lists of words won't do at all.

Infants Need Talk, Talk, Talk

NEWBORNS HAVE A repertoire of skills for dissecting patterns and sounds in speech, and they are universal (biological). The skills work in exactly the same way, regardless of the language. But although the skills are the same, the languages are not, and one of baby's main tasks in the first year of life is to figure out what is special about his particular language that he is supposed to notice and remember. He can only do that if he hears this language as much as possible. The sky's the limit.

Mothers have a jump start on engaging their infants' attention in conversations. The sound patterns and rhythms in *The Cat in the Hat* are not the only kind of things that babies can remember from being in the womb. They also remember your voice, even though it sounds a little different outside the womb than it did inside it. Babies like your voice so much that they will suck on a special (electrically wired) pacifier to turn it on—and won't suck to turn on another woman's voice. [The sucking reflex is a major tool in infant research. Infants suck when they like something, and they will suck in order to get something to happen.] Not only does baby like your voice, but he likes *you* so much he'll be able to recognize your face only a week after he is born, and he'll prefer to look at your face rather than someone else's.

Babies Mind Not Getting Their Turn

ALMOST AT BIRTH, infants have the rudiments of a conversational style, which will blossom in a few weeks or so. They will move in rhythm as you speak and gaze into your face. When they are a little older, at around six weeks, they will light up with a bright smile at the sound of your voice. They will take turns and expect you to do the same. As your voice drops in pitch at the end of a few phrases, then it's their turn, and they mind if you don't let them have it. At first, 'their turn' might consist of an intent look, a sudden jerk of a limb, and a grunt or two, but that's the best they can do, and they mean every inch of it.

Scottish psychologists did a fascinating study that proves babies really do care about their role in this rhythmic dance. They filmed mothers in conversation with their young infants. The infant's reactions to mom's soothing voice and her forward and backward rhythmic movements were remarkable. When mom swayed closer, so did baby. The babies locked on to their mom's eyes like a radar gun each time she made eye contact. When mom gazed at and spoke directly to her infant, she got a bright smile in return. When her voice dropped in cadence and she paused slightly, the baby would fill the pause with an *ooh* or a wiggled fist.

Next, on a different day, the babies were treated to a replay of the mother's portion of the film as they sat propped up on a little chair. At the sight of mom, the baby's face lit up like a ray of sunshine with a broad, bright smile. As the seconds ticked by, the baby would interject a gurgle or a happy grunt. But now, mom's responses no longer fit with what her baby did. The baby's smile lingered, then slowly faded. His eyes opened wider. He stared harder. Each time baby tried to take a turn, mom's patterns of behavior and her timing were completely unrelated to what the baby did. The infant's sober, quizzical stare turned somber. The corners of his mouth drooped toward his chin. His brow furrowed. It wasn't long before he started to wail and had to be rescued.

This is the scientific proof that babies care about their role in this conversational dance, and it's also an explanation for why some mothers don't get the happy reactions they expect from their infants. The critical message is: *Tune in to your baby's behavior.*

From around the third month, baby's conversational turn begins to look smoother, is more coordinated, and contains lots of *uhs*, *goos*, and *coos*. Conversational turn-taking will continue through babbling, through the stage of one-word phrases and 'telegraphic speech,' through the first halting stage of sentences, and on into adult life. People who never learned the trick of taking turns listening and speaking, or perhaps had it thwarted in childhood, don't have many friends.

Most mothers react spontaneously and appropriately to

these conversations, but some mothers aren't aware that baby has an intention too. Monitor your own behavior and watch what you do. Do you give baby a chance to respond? Do you wait a little after you've spoken awhile so baby can have a turn? Do you acknowledge whatever it is that baby is trying to express, even if it's just a twitch or a grunt? Babies love it when you respond directly to them, repeating what they just said as if it actually meant something. "*Ugh!* Well that's a beautiful grunt." Mothers clearly have their infant's attention in these conversations. Don't waste it. (I promise not to use *don't* very often in this book, but when I do, I mean it.)

Keep Your Voice Up and the Noise Down

BABIES LEARN A LANGUAGE by engaging in mutual, social interactions while listening to what you and other family members say. They focus best in a quiet, calm environment without distractions. In fact, they can't hear at all if the background noise is too loud. They need what engineers call a high 'signal-to-noise ratio,' a huge boost from the signal (your voice) to hear it over background sounds. Infants are particularly vulnerable to background noise, and to a lesser extent, so are toddlers and children up to the age of ten, one reason why your requests may go unheeded.

This means you should turn off the radio or TV when talking to your infant. And here's another 'don't,' about TVs, radios, and telephones. Babies need verbal stimulation, but babies are social creatures. They need conversations *with you*, or with dad or a sibling, so they know that talk has something to do with them. Up to the age of three, children won't learn anything about language from sitting in front of a television set or watching *Mary Poppins*, nor will they learn by overhearing a conversation you're having on the phone or over a cup of coffee with a friend. Babies learn when you are talking *to them*. Three-year-olds might learn something from TV *if you watch with them*, pointing out what's going on, asking questions to see if they notice things.

I should also add here that if you have to put your infant in day care, make sure the ratio of children to the number of staff is satisfactory for the age of your child. Ask very particular questions about how much time the staff spends interacting and talking one-on-one with each infant. For a very young infant, this should be a major part of his waking time. Make one or two unexpected visits if you can.

Mix and Match

MATCHING SIGHT AND MOVEMENT

The amazing language learning machine, your child, comes into the world with a variety of special equipment, rather like a carpenter's belt of tools. Not only can she recognize something she has heard before, like your voice, but she can do something that seems quite impossible. Try this little experiment. Get your baby's attention, then stick out your tongue as far as it will go and leave it there. Baby will copy you. Or if you don't like sticking out your tongue to your sweet baby, then open your mouth wide as though you've just won the lottery and stand there. Baby will copy you.

No one knows how babies do this, but it means that *at birth* the visual system in the brain is wired up to the motor parts that control the muscles of the face, tongue, and jaw. After all, there is no way that baby can see her own face. She can't look down at her mouth over those bulgy cheeks to check if she's doing it right. There has to be a link between what she sees you do and a 'motor map' of how to do it created by the visual input. This gives us a clue that baby is wired up to watch your mouth move while you speak, and this will be important later when she starts to say her first wordlike noises. All the more reason why it's important to look at your baby while you talk to her—and be sure you are in her range of clearest focus, about a foot away.

Infants automatically see in 3-D nearly at birth, but stereo-acuity, the ability to see detail in depth, has to be wired up by the brain when it gets input from each eye. This ability is advancing rapidly at around the fifth month. Stereo-acuity helps us do things like put the cap on the toothpaste tube or notice which leaves on a tree are clearly in front of or behind others. Try this experiment. Cover one eye with your hand. Walk around like that for a while. Then focus on something like the leaves on a nearby tree. Now take your hand away and notice the difference.

If your child's eyes frequently drift out of alignment (lazy eye) or one eye looks dull and unfocused, and the eyes stay that way for long periods of time, the brain will wire up a world that is misaligned and blurry. Eventually one eye dominates completely and the input from the other eye is suppressed. This can happen early, so be sure to have your child examined by a pediatric optometrist or ophthalmologist. Once one eye is fully suppressed it will stay that way, and your child will see the world like you did in the experiment above for the rest of his life.

Newborns can't see color very well. They *can* see bright, bold primary colors, but actually prefer high-contrast black and white stripes. Color vision starts to develop early, however, and after a few months it is nearly as good as an adult's.

MATCHING SIGHT AND SOUND

The visual-motor talent is matched by a visual-auditory talent that is just as remarkable. In one study, the experimenters played a video of an object moving up and down in a fixed rhythm. At the same time, a loud speaker relayed a tape recording of a sound (boink, boink, boink) that either matched the rhythm of the moving object or did not. Newborns preferred to look at the video that matched the rhythm of the sound. They showed their preference by the sucking technique described above. All of us have a sense of extreme discomfort when the audio portion of a movie is out of synch with the actors' mouth movements. Infants do as well, particularly if the video is a film of mommy talking.

MATCHING SOUND AND SOUND

I have already described how newborns can tell their mother's voice from a stranger's voice, and scientists have pinned down exactly how they do it. It certainly isn't what she is saying, because newborns have no way to understand words. Instead, it is the quality of her voice (the timbre), her vocal inflection or prosody (shifts in pitch), and the natural rhythmic stress of her speech. These cues are so powerful that within a few days of life, infants can tell the difference between the rhythm and intonation of their own language versus a foreign language, especially if the stress patterns are noticeably different. This is another reason why it is important that infants hear whole phrases and sentences and not repeated words.

The Amazing Language Learning Machine

A Tiny Chisel in the Tool Kit

AS WE SAW EARLIER, unborn babies can tell when two syllables reverse: *baby* to *beebay*. More refined tests have shown that after birth they can even do better. They can tell syllables apart by a change in only one sound. They can hear the difference between a *ba* and a *pa*, for example. Since this pioneering study appeared in 1971, scientists have thrown the phonetic book at newborns, trying out all possible combinations and permutations of simple consonant-vowel syllables to discover what the infant can and can't hear and compare.

They do this by training the infant to listen to one particular syllable. *Ba-ba-ba-ba* is played over a loudspeaker until the infant gets bored and stops sucking on the pacifier. Even newborns get bored with too much repetition. When baby stops playing the game, a new sound *pa-pa-pa-pa* is presented, and everyone waits to see if the infant will notice the difference and start playing the game again (sucking again). He always does.

In this way, it was discovered that babies are amazingly good at this. They can tell consonants apart that differ in 'voicing.' *Ba* differs from *pa* in only one feature: the vocal cords vibrate immediately with *ba*, but start 40 milliseconds later with *pa*. One millisecond is 1/1000th of a second. Newborns have no trouble with other consonant contrasts, whether they differ by place of articulation (*ba* versus *ga*—*ba* is made with the lips, *ga* with the back of the tongue), by blocking air through the nose or not (*ma* versus *wa*), by stopping the flow of air or not (*ba* versus *za*), or any other speech contrasts that linguists care to toss at them. And, the consonants don't have to come at the front of the syllable. Newborns do just as well when they come at the end (*ap*, *ab*), and they do equally well telling vowels apart.

Why Chinese Babies Can Learn Chinese

So far we've seen that English babies can tell English sounds apart at birth, and as some of these pioneering studies were done in Paris, we know that French babies can tell French sounds apart. Well, you might say, this is not so remarkable, because baby has been listening to mom for three months in the womb. This is plenty of time to pick up all forty or so sounds in the English language. If learning is the key to this skill, then our little bundle of joy is going to fail miserably with foreign language sounds that don't exist in his own language. Languages have scores of vocal noises to choose among, and no language comes close to using them all.

Imagine everyone's surprise when it was discovered that within the first week of life, newborns can distinguish between all the sounds in every language in the world, no matter how unusual they are. Scientists have compared newborns' ability first with their own language, and then with alien sounds from another language. Babies were tested on contrasting European languages, on a European language versus a language of distant peoples like Hindi or Japanese, or on exotic languages like Zulu and Nthlakapmx (an Indian language from the Pacific northwest). Infants were tested on speech sounds as strange as Zulu medial and lateral clicks, and the Ethiopian 'ejective place of articulation' distinction. The babies came up trumps, no matter where they lived and which language they had been exposed to.

Well, no wonder Chinese babies can learn Chinese, Indian babies can learn Hindi, and South African babies can learn Zulu! Babies are primed to learn every language that exists or ever existed. Does this mean that they have a 'special language processor module' in the brain? A lot of people think so, and a lot of people don't. We'll talk more about this shortly.

Meanwhile, something wasn't quite right. Whether or not our brains have an inbuilt language processor or just a very sensitive auditory system for analyzing all the sounds in all the languages of the world, people ought to retain this talent throughout their lives. Adults should do just as well telling these alien language noises apart as babies do. But it turns out that adults are complete dunces at this task. If babies are experts and adults are dunces, then when does duncehood begin? This took a while to find out—back to age ten (dunce), then to age four (dunce), age two (dunce), age one (dunce), age six months (expert), now forward in time to nine months (expert). We now know that infants' apparently infinite repertoire of sound sensitivities starts to diminish toward the end of the first year. At around twelve months, the ability to hear alien sounds in foreign languages appears to have totally evaporated.

Or has it? A newborn's sensitivity to speech contrasts is one of the most replicable findings in infant research. There is scarcely a study that doesn't confirm this universal skill in the young infant, and the fact that it disappears by twelve months. Yet this doesn't make sense, for the simple reason that, as everybody knows, two-year-olds, five-year-olds, and most children up until about the age of eight can learn a foreign language without a trace of an accent. How is this possible if they are 'deaf' to nonnative sounds in that language? Common sense tells us that if the ability to hear and tell apart all the sounds of all the languages in the world goes away completely, second language learning would be impossible unless you started teaching it during the first year of life. A child who was adopted from a foreign land, could never learn a new language after the age of one.

One current hypothesis to explain this paradox, goes like this: As infants hear more and more of the sounds of their own language, the ability to hear alien sounds begins to 'go unconscious.' This happens because the infant's job is to pay attention to and remember *only the sounds that matter* so she can eventually produce them. But this auditory skill isn't lost completely. It slowly withers over time for lack of exposure, becoming harder and harder to recover. The sooner a second language is taught, the better. This is a kind of use-it-or-lose-it model, but all it does is invent a story to describe the data. It doesn't prove or explain anything. What does 'go unconscious' mean? Is it really necessary for this aptitude to go unconscious? Why shouldn't we possess this skill throughout our lives? Right now, your guess is as good as anyone else's.

Why the Brain Makes Categories

HERE IS ANOTHER MYSTERY. Researchers have known for over forty years that adults exhibit what is known as categorical perception. Imagine a computer program that gradually turns one consonant-vowel sequence into another in equal steps, slowly turning *ba* into *pa*. The computer stores a record of the acoustic properties of both *ba* and *pa*, then alters whatever it is that makes them different so they change slowly into each other. Can people hear this slow shift from *ba* to *pa*? Not on your life. They hear either *ba* or *pa*. When newborns are tested, they behave just like adults. Instead of hearing a series of different *ba*'s slowly turning into a series of different *pa*'s, they hear *ba-ba-ba-ba-ba* and then suddenly *pa-pa-pa-pa*. Sounds closer to a *ba* are heard as a clear *ba*, and sounds closer to *pa* are heard as a clear *pa*. The brain insists on filing these sounds into two categories and no more. (Categorical perception happens with most consonant contrasts but much less so for vowels.) The only difference between the adults and the newborns is that the infants have categorical perception for speech contrasts in all languages of the world. Adults can't even tell the sounds apart.

Obviously, categorical perception can't be due to prolonged exposure to speech, as people used to believe. It is due to something that is wired up at birth, something that has to be helpful to a species that uses language. It starts to make sense when you think about it. We can understand speech through various kinds of distortions. We can understand what people are saying whether they speak slowly or quickly, whether they speak loudly or whisper, whether they are a man, woman, or child, and even when they speak in a different dialect (providing it isn't too extreme). Anything sounding remotely like *b* will be heard as *b*, or for newborns, anything sounding remotely like an Ethiopian ejective place of articulation contrast, will be heard as that too. Whatever system exists in the brain, clearly it is a 'sloppy tuning device,' the opposite of what a good violinist tries to be. Anything that is *sort of* like a *b* is good enough for us. This is the reason why computer speech recognition devices have been such a dismal failure. Computers demand precision: one particular voice, saying a limited set of words, slowly and clearly. Babies and the rest of us don't need this precision. Anybody's talk will do.

Scientists are scratching their heads about the results of the infant studies. If there is some kind of program in the brain that makes infants *better than adults* at telling language sounds apart, yet the *same as adults* in categorical perception, what sort of program could this be? This is a very controversial issue. It could be that these aptitudes are part and parcel of an excellent general purpose auditory system, not specific to language but sensitive to all kinds of sounds. There is some support for this idea from studies on fine judgments of musical sounds that vary in pitch and timing. Infants can make these fine judgments as well as adults, at least those adults without musical training. Other support comes from animal research. Monkeys, and even chinchillas and Japanese quail, can distinguish simple syllables like *ba* and *pa*. What is more remarkable is that their categorical perception is similar to ours. The big difference is that it takes hundreds and even thousands of learning trials for this effect to appear, while human infants can do this within a few minutes.

The opposing theory is that we possess a special language processing module—a processor in the brain entirely devoted to language. It sits in the left hemisphere of the human brain (and in no other brains). This processor has special cells (neurons) that resonate only to sounds in speech. It has unique brain operators that direct the newborn's attention to specific patterns in coherent speech, which drive the infant toward language acquisition. It also houses a grammar acquisition device.

It's going to take a while to sort this out.

Tools That Need Time to Work Properly

Marching to the Beat

NOT EVERYTHING is given to the infant on a plate. Much of the work is still to come. Babies have a great jump start, but they are faced with the awesome task of finding out what a word is and unplugging it from a stream of speech. Up to now I have been talking about what infants can do in highly controlled experiments where they hear one sound or syllable at a time. Their skills are truly amazing, but by themselves they aren't nearly enough.

The stress pattern of the language is one of the first clues infants rely on to unplug words. In English, the majority of words, especially common words, have the stress on the first syllable: *bá-by, tá-ble, dín-ner*, as do people's names: Jénn-y, Jóhnn-y, Phýll-is, Éd-ward, Géoff-rey, Jú-lie, and so on. By emphasizing the stress patterns in your speech, you can help your baby with this task. Babies hear and remember rhythmic speech patterns in the womb, but they need a lot of exposure to a particular language to discover its precise stress patterns. They start to become experts at around six months of age, not only for stress patterns, but also for inflection. Inflection is a rise or fall in pitch to signal a pause, a question, or a speaker turn. Specific stress or emphasis (louder, slower) is often placed on the most important word in a phrase to signify meaning, and this marks a word clearly as a word. For example, "Where did *you* go today?" implies that you weren't supposed to go anywhere, and yet you did, but didn't tell anyone. "Where did you *go* today?" implies that everyone knew you were going somewhere, like to the store, but the speaker now wants specifics. "Where did you go *today*?" asks where you went today, not yesterday or last week.

Using All the Tools at Once

SOMETIME BETWEEN SIX AND NINE months, infants begin to use all their tools at once, rather like a carpenter with ten arms. They use their sense of the overall rhythm of the language, voice inflection, plus their new knowledge of the stress patterns, to isolate what might be words. Then they focus on the wordiness aspects to check it out. Every language has a unique syllable structure. This means that certain sounds are 'legal' in one order but not in another. Certain consonants can come in a row, and others cannot. A syllable structure is legal regardless of whether a word exists in the language. The nonsense word *storch* is perfectly legal in English, but *nteebl* is not, even though it is completely pronounceable. In English, *nt* is legal at the ends of words but not at the beginning, and *bl* is legal at the beginnings of words but not at the end. Linguists call this structure of sounds within syllables *phonotactics*. Infants have solved the phonotactic structure of their native language by nine months of age, and by ten or eleven months they have no trouble handling all the cues at once with equal facility: stress patterns for both strong/weak (*prét-ty*) and weak/strong syllables (*a-roúnd*), word emphasis, inflection, pausing, and phonotactic cues.

With a little help from you, infants can jump the gun. One study showed that infants only eight months old could detect a word embedded in a story after they had heard the word repeated several times. And they can do this backwards. That is, if they hear a story with a word that repeats a lot, they can show afterwards that they recognize this word in a list of words. Remember this is strictly word detection practice; it has nothing to do with understanding what words are or what they mean.

Infants pay attention, infinite attention, but they don't solve the word problem by consciously deploying their tools. They don't think, *Today, I'm going to spend some time doing word work*. The tools work automatically, rather like a vacuum cleaner when you plug it in and switch it on. If dirt is there, the vacuum will scoop it up. The vacuum is designed to 'focus' on floors. Babies are designed to focus on us and what we say. They can't help it. That's the way their equipment was built. All you have to do to get baby's attention and turn on baby's language machine, is to start talking. And all you have to do to keep baby's attention, is to keep talking, making sure that you let baby have a turn too.

The perceptual systems in the human and animal brain work by a simple principle: They automatically extract and code *recurring patterns* from complex input. By *patterns*, I mean whatever has structure. A memory trace is activated and strengthened every time the same pattern appears, and the more often it occurs the more it will be remembered. A pattern can appear in many contexts, the more the merrier. You can recognize Mr. Sylvester, the man in the corner grocery store, each time you see him, without any effort whatsoever. And you can recognize him whether he's facing you, looking out the window, or standing sideways. You can recognize him at the fireworks display in the park, even if you don't immediately recall where you saw him before, who he is, or what his name is, until you think about it for a while. This is because the brain files not only the pattern (Mr. Sylvester's face), but also the pattern in a context (the grocery store).

Perceptual systems extract information about regularities, or invariances, in the input. This is what infants' brains are doing when they hear speech, and each brain will find the regular patterns in speech effortlessly, without any help from us. Nevertheless, infants must attend to something for the perceptual systems to work, and they can't operate at all unless there is something to attend to. In order for an infant's word-extracting tools to develop, he needs someone to grab his attention (your face and voice, or somebody else's), plus hundreds of hours of conversations. This is the only way it works. There isn't any shortcut.

Words, Words, Words

Babbling

WHILE THE INFANT has been paying close attention to these speech sounds, she has been working overtime to figure out how to produce them. At seven or eight months, babbling begins. It starts as repetitive sequences of those famous consonant-vowel syllables, *ba-ba-ba-ba*, and then gradually gets fancier with time, *ba-ma-ba, ta-ta-pa.* Linguists used to think that babies babble in all the languages of the world, but scientific research proved they don't. Babbling includes the sounds, stress patterns, and inflections of the native language. This means that hearing spoken language is critical to kick-start babbling. Younger babies may blow raspberries, make some incredible noises, and may even string together a coo and a squeak, but this isn't babbling. Babbling is conscious, controlled practice with sounds of the native language. It is baby's first attempt at talking, of trying to do directly what you do, and out of this effort comes true speech. Most (not all) babies' first word appears at about one year of age.

If babbling depends on hearing spoken language, what about children who are born deaf? Experts once believed that babbling was a 'linguistic universal'—it always came in on cue regardless of the input. But this isn't true. Deaf children do babble, but they start much later, somewhere between eleven and twenty-five months. They make a very limited range of sounds, not necessarily those found in their native language. Because they can't hear the sounds as they make them (there is no auditory feedback), this babbling effort doesn't last long. However, deaf babies do 'babble' through gesture and hand movements. It is common to see a deaf infant manually 'babbling,' even when she is alone in a crib. This is one reason why some experts believe it's important to teach a deaf baby sign language as early as possible.

Understanding What a Word Is

EARLIER WE SAW that little Jenny could recognize her name at four and a half months. Jenny didn't *know* that this was *her* name, or even that it was a name. She had heard it a lot, usually in a warm, fuzzy context. It sounded familiar. It was a pattern of sounds that the brain automatically extracted from the speech stream, and coded and filed it. It is another matter for babies to understand that a word can represent something, someone, or an event. Making this connection is a major milestone, because it is the first glimmer of symbolic reasoning. A group of meaningless noises *can stand for something real.* This understanding doesn't begin until babbling is underway. Babbling is a kind of litmus test that the child is ready to link speech sounds to something out there in the world.

Until recently, researchers believed that infants didn't begin to understand that words referred to something in the world until they were around nine months old. In 1999, the clock was pushed back to six months. In this study, baby sat on mom's lap facing side-by-side videos of mom and dad who had been filmed earlier while they were watching a movie. After the babies got used to looking at the videos, a neutral voice said *mommy* or *daddy*. The infants looked most often at the video that matched the word. When mom and dad were replaced by videos of a strange man and woman, infants didn't show the same behavior. In other words, the six-month-olds treated *mommy* and *daddy* as names for particular people, not names for men and women in general.

Making Sense of Baby's Babbles

YOU CAN SPEED this process along by making sense of the babbles for your baby. This means 'making sense' in the literal meaning, connecting the spoken sounds to something seen, felt, or experienced. If baby says, *ma-ma-ma-ma*, smile broadly, pick her up, look her in the eye, and pat yourself. Pick up her hand and put it on your face. Say, "*Yes! Mama*," repeatedly. Or if baby says, *da-da-da-da*, carry her to daddy, have her pat daddy while you say, "*This is Daddy*," repeatedly. The more excitement the better. In other words, acknowledge her attempt to talk as if she was saying real words, just as you pretended in your 'junior conversations' that blowing a raspberry was a real word. Be sure to make the connection between words that *sound like* the name of something. Don't assign *ga-ga-ga* to Robespierre the dog. Be consistent, so that the same babble you raved about on Tuesday, is acknowledged on Thursday and assigned to the same person, object, or event. Repetition is the key to everything. I should add, that most mothers spontaneously do what I have just described.

Social context and emotion are two important ingredients for building a vocabulary—how exciting, interesting, comforting is whatever it is that baby wants to remember and talk about. That is why when little Alex says, *wa-wa-wa-wa*, it might not be that meaningful to waltz him down a flight of stairs, into the laundry room, pat the washing machine and say, "*Wa-wa-wa-waaaah-shing*." Of course, Alex might be fascinated by the washing machine, in which case taking that detour to the laundry room could be a good idea, especially if the machine is sloshing or whizzing noisily around.

The safer choice is to focus on the immediate surroundings and the context of what you are doing together. If you are in the kitchen, baby in high chair having lunch on a rather hot day, you could make a connection with *wa-wa-wa* by turning on the tap and offering her a cup of water, saying animatedly, *waaah-ter* a few times. If the infant's *wa-wa-wa* is consistently rewarded with a cup of water, then he learns how to use words to gain control, to produce an effect in the environment. The *wa-wa-wa* could mean something quite different. It might be an announcement that baby has pulled himself to a standing position with the help of the coffee table. Use this too: "*Oh, look*" (a familiar phrase by now), "*Timmy is waaaah-king.*" As you try to link up speech sounds to meaning, remember that for your infant, meaning is likely to be a whole event: the *act* of mom getting a cup of water; *the act* of pulling himself up from a sitting position to a standing position, in the living room, with the aid of *that* coffee table. (It could work again!)

Infants Understand More than They Say

THE EMOTIONAL ASPECTS of a baby's experience, those things connected with persons, events, and objects, are a major factor in determining which words your child understands first. Several studies and surveys have been carried out to find out what words babies understand, and when, before they speak. Around nine or ten months babies can show you that they know quite a bit. They know the names of everyone in the family, and probably the dog or cat's name too. And they know the words of their favorite foods (juice, cookie), favorite toys, and types of clothing. *Shoe* seems to have a special place in infants' hearts.

Infants also know the names of common events, routines, and games (things that occur regularly, have a sequence and a goal). They know words like *lunch, bath, bye-bye, bed,* and *peekaboo.* Infants give these words a very broad meaning. 'Event words' wrap an entire drama. To an infant, *bath* means: (1) go with mom or dad, (2) watch the tub fill up, (3) clothes come off, (4) get put into tub, (5) play with water and toys, (6) get soaped up, (7) get rinsed off, (8) get dried off, powdered, and diapered, (9) get put into pajamas. Getting into bed, the next action, may get tacked on to the meaning of *bath.* Or the word *bed* may start with the pajamas part, then include being put into bed, the story, the tucking in, the hug and kiss, and the disappearance of mom or dad, with or without the night-light left on. Notice what your infant does *first* when you say one of these event words.

Babies try earnestly to communicate at about nine months although they have no words. They will babble something, directing their gaze intently in the direction of what they want. If they have mastered the trick of pointing, which many do during the period between nine and twelve months, they will point as well. In other words, babies can signal a request. And they will let you know in no uncertain terms when they don't want something to happen. They do this by shaking their head, or turning away, and some can even muster a *no*.

How well do mothers do in interpreting their baby's first attempts to communicate? Studies show that mothers work very hard at interpretation: "Do you want some milk? Do you want a cracker? Do you want some juice? Do you want to get down?" For every wrong answer, there is feedback in the form of a whine, a head shake, or a *no*. Then the infant tries harder, stretching forward, pointing more carefully, vocalizing more loudly. On average, mothers have a 50/50 chance of getting it right the first time around. But mother and baby don't give up, and only 5 percent of these exchanges end in failure. Moms work hard until they succeed, even when what the infant wants is utterly unpredictable. In one observational study, the item was a bath sponge lying amidst food, plates, and utensils on the kitchen counter.

Babies clearly have a hard time making themselves understood, but they are remarkably better at understanding what you're saying to them. When dad responds, "Do you want milk?" the baby knows exactly what he means, and can nod, or shake his head, or whine in frustration. In a large survey, thousands of mothers were asked to check off the words their babies understood from a long list of common words. Detailed checks were made against the parents' reports and their child's true ability, and the estimates based on mother's knowledge were confirmed as accurate. The findings showed that by ten months, the infants understood around 40 words, quite impressive. But word knowledge varied enormously from 11 words for the bottom 10 percent of the infants to 154 words for the top 10 percent. By sixteen months, rather than narrowing, this gap had widened, showing that the children who lagged behind had not caught up. At this age, the average was 169 words, with the bottom 10 percent scoring 92 words and the top 10 percent 321. One reason for these discrepancies, apart from chronic middle ear infections, and the occasional late bloomer, is the quantity and quality of speech to the child. And, of course, this speech doesn't have to come only from the mother; dad, grandparents, brothers and sisters, and a sensitive baby minder will do just as well.

How Many Words Are Enough Words?

PART OF THE REASON why some infants understand more words than others do is simply because there are natural differences in infants' developmental rate of language; it doesn't have much to do with parenting. The evidence of this striking variability between children is most clear in measures of spoken vocabulary, which I will discuss in the next chapter.

But there is much more going on than developmental rate. A remarkable study was carried out by Betty Hart and Todd Risley. They had been working with children enrolled in Head Start, a government-sponsored program for preschoolers who have been deprived in childhood by poverty and other hardships. Hart and Risley became frustrated by the fact that it was hard to make a noticeable difference in the children's language skills, and they felt sure the reason was due to a problem that must start earlier in the children's life.

They decided to study parent-child interactions when children were much younger. The families were videotaped for one hour every month when the children were between the ages of nine months and three years. Ultimately, forty-two children and their families made it to the end of the study. Thirteen families were from the highest socioeconomic group, designated *professional*. Twenty-three families were *middle class,* and six families were on *welfare*. The focus was on the child's spoken vocabulary, and on how parents (usually the mother) spoke to their child.

The parents' communications were scored for the number of words per hour, and for simple counts of nouns, adjectives, past tense verbs, and 'wh' questions used in each session. Hart and Risley also categorized the mother's style of verbal interaction with her infant. They tallied the number of imperatives (demands), statements of approval and disapproval, positive and negative feedback, and so forth. In the final analysis, these measures were grouped into six categories:

1. *language diversity*: number of different nouns and modifiers

2. *positive feedback tone*: repetitions, extensions, expansions, confirmations, praise, approval

3. *negative feedback tone*: imperatives, prohibitions, disconfirmations, criticisms, disparagements

4. *symbolic emphasis*: the degree to which parents made connections between things and events as indicated by richness of nouns, modifiers, and number of past tense verbs

5. *guidance style*: the number of invitations—"Shall we?"—divided by the number of imperatives—"Stop it."

6. *responsiveness*: the number of responses to the child—"Oh, you want Mommy to take the ball"— divided by the number of initiations to the child— "Why don't you play with your blocks?"

There were enormous differences between the high/middle/ low socioeconomic groups just in terms of mothers' sheer verbal output to their children. The average number of words per hour addressed to the child between the ages of thirteen and thirty-six months, was over 2,000 for moms in the professional group, 1,250 for the middle-class group, and 616 for the welfare mothers. This happened even though the welfare mothers spent, overall, more time in the same room with the child.

There were differences, as well, as a function of the child's age. Professional mothers not only talked much more to their *babies* (1500 words per hour between nine and twelve months), but this increased systematically with the child's age, leveling off by thirty months at around 2,500 words per hour. The middle-class parents spoke less overall, and their initial rate was lower and increased more modestly (1,000–1,500 words). The range for the welfare mothers was virtually nonexistent (600–750 words). Based on these numbers, it was estimated that by age three, a child from a professional family would have heard 33 million words; a middle-class child, 20 million; and a child of a welfare mother, 9 million.

But this didn't tell the whole story. The three groups were noticeably different in the way mothers interacted with their children. Professional mothers used a much richer vocabulary. Interactions with their children were consistently positive, at twice the rate of middle-class mothers, and five times the rate of welfare mothers. They rarely used negative feedback of any type. They were highly responsive and far less inclined to be directive.

Middle-class parents were "similar but less so" in terms of the positive measures. Welfare mothers had a very different style of verbal interaction with their children. Almost 80 percent of the feedback to the child was negative and prohibitive (Stop it. What did I tell you? Put that back or else. I said no!). They frequently discouraged or disparaged their youngsters, calling them stupid or dumb. Encouragement was rare, and sometimes absent altogether. This didn't mean that mothers on welfare were cruel and didn't love their children. They were just as affectionate as the professional and middle-class mothers, and met their baby's needs.

The children's vocabulary development was strongly related to the sheer *quantity* of the words they heard. At age three, children in professional families had an average spoken vocabulary of 1,115 words (true count); middle-class children, 750 words; and children of welfare mothers, 525. Middle-class and welfare children were not that far apart, yet, by now, differences in IQ between the groups were huge. Average IQ scores measured at age three, were 117, 107, and 79 (100 is average).

However, there was a problem with this study. There's no way to know how much the results were a consequence of the mother's (and father's) verbal IQ. We know that verbal ability is highly heritable, though environment plays an equally important role. If professional moms had higher verbal IQs, which is likely, this means they would be more verbal—talk a lot, use a more complex vocabulary, and handle the interaction with their child more sensitively (more 'intelligently'). There is certainly evidence for this interpretation. The vocabulary scores of the mothers were strongly correlated to their children's actual (recorded) vocabulary and to their children's IQ, support for the effect of heredity.

But heredity is not destiny. When Hart and Risley looked at the quality and character of the mothers' interactions with their children, this turned out to be more important than the parents' vocabulary. All six categories of parenting style were highly predictive of the child's vocabulary, IQ score, and performance on general language tests at age three. Not only this, but the parents' communicative style predicted their children's language skills almost as well when they were followed up at age nine.

Although mom's communicative style can't be completely disentangled from her verbal IQ, we *can* see the impact of her style on her child's language development. There is certainly no reason why any parent can't copy what works best. Here's the list:

1. The sheer *quantity* of parents' verbal output (total number of words per hour) predicts a child's spoken vocabulary later in time. This is simply a numbers game: The more you say, the more words your child will learn.

2. The *quality* of communicative style (its richness, and the type of feedback the child receives) were stronger predictors of the child's verbal development than social class. This was seen in the data for individual children where social class mattered far less than how the mother interacted with her infant. This means that your child's facility with language—how articulate they become—depends on both the complexity of your language and the sensitivity with which you interact with your child.

3. Five key communicative styles have been identified that greatly enhance language skills for as long as they have been measured, which is up to age nine. These are, in order of importance:

> **guidance style.** Provide gentle invitations to play and
> engage in positive interactions. Avoid prohibitions.
> **symbolic emphasis.** Make connections between words
> and things and other words.
> **feedback tone.** Positive feedback is good; negative feedback is bad.

language diversity. Use different nouns, verbs, adjectives as much as possible.

responsiveness. Tune in. Follow baby's lead. Don't order baby around.

When Communication Breaks Down: Behaviors to Avoid

OTHER SHORT-TERM STUDIES have shown that, by and large, most mothers have highly appropriate responses to their infant's fledgling communications. However, certain patterns of interactions have been shown to cause communication to break down or never begin at all. Mothers and their infants were studied for three months, starting when the babies were nine months old. Communication patterns were carefully observed over the three-month period. The infant's spoken vocabulary was measured at thirteen months. Four inappropriate styles of communication were discovered, which caused the baby's contribution to diminish or stop.

1. *Ignoring or failing to pay attention to your infant.* This type of mother was characterized as 'otherwise occupied' due to being depressed, tired, or worried, or because she was selfish and indifferent. "Ignoring" in this sense did not mean neglect. Mothers met their baby's basic needs.

2. *Dominating the interaction, being generally intrusive.* The mother wants the infant to do what she want him to do, no matter what the infant wants to do. She constantly interferes, taking away a toy and substituting another one, imposing her will. When the infant tries to initiate an interaction, she initiates a different one. From the infant's perspective, this mother isn't taking turns or respecting the infant's turn. This makes play and any kind of communication impossible.

3. *Using prohibitions excessively.* Don't! Stop that! Watch out! Don't break it! This tells the infant what *not* to do and never what *to do.* Prohibitions block action and communication. Prohibitions, in and of themselves, aren't the problem (all mothers need to alert their children to potential danger). As Hart and Risley found in their observations, it's the *amount* and the degree of negativity that are the problem. Excessive prohibitions tend to go hand in hand with an abnormal lack of positive feedback. These infants rarely hear happy voices full of praise: How nice! Aren't you smart! What a sweetie pie! This is a double whammy.

4. *Failing to engage an inattentive, passive infant in a conversation or an activity.* The infant who sits daydreaming or dozing off due to boredom isn't learning much. This pattern is common among parents who 'park' their child in a baby container for long periods of time so they can get on with something else. Children who are by nature uncomplaining or passive are the most easily parked. Yet these are the very children who should NOT be shut out this way. As an aside, modern baby containers, though more colorful (and noisy) are often highly constraining, limiting baby to only one type of movement. The old-fashioned wooden playpen was much more child-friendly. It was large enough for baby to roll over and crawl around. Its wooden slats provided a good handhold for pulling up to a standing position. The rail around the top was a good support for walking. Babies of all ages need complete freedom of movement to practice their fine-motor and gross-motor skills.

In the study above, when the children's vocabularies were measured at thirteen months, the results were clear. Infants with mothers who responded appropriately had larger vocabularies. The vocabularies of the infants with mothers who had one or more of the styles listed above were well below normal.

A Parent's Guide

Minding Your Style

As WE HAVE SEEN, not only is the *amount* of talk important for a child to learn language, but the *quality* of the interaction and the *sensitivity* and *effort* mom and dad make to interpret their infant's requests are equally important. Here are some helpful suggestions for what you might do to make the most of your interaction with your child during his or her first year of life.

Parents should take full advantage of Hart and Risley's important discoveries. Infants need an almost nonstop verbal barrage delivered from parents who use all five of the important communicative styles *at the same time*. This may be a tall order for some parents, while other parents may feel they're already doing what is appropriate. My suggestion is for everyone to monitor their verbal interactions with their infants for about a week or so, and check on this from time to time as the child grows older. We are awfully bad observers of our own behavior unless we deliberately focus our attention on it. Some of you will pass with perfect scores, but most parents can do with a little tune-up. Other parents will want to drastically change their ways, especially if they are using the wrong communicative style *and* have a cranky and difficult child. It's remarkable how parenting style influences a child's mood and behavior.

Here are some suggestions for how to carry out a productive check on your own styles of communication. When you get baby up from a nap, watch what you do. Do you pick him up, give him a hug, change his diaper and/or clothes, all in silence? (I have seen mothers do this.) Or do you take this opportunity to fill his head with talk and to generate some basic kind of conversation—like this:

"Oh, Timmy just woke up!! Did you have a nice nap? Do you want to get up and come with Mommy *[or Daddy]*?" *[Wait for eye contact. Give baby a chance to answer your question, even if he can only say yes by a change of expression.]* "Oh, you do! Well, let's see if Mommy can pick Timmy up. Oh my goodness, what a big, heavy boy you are."

"Well hello, little Timmy. Can you say hello to Mommy? Can you say hi?" *[Wait.]* "Are you still sleepy?" *[Wait.]* "Let's see if you need changing. Uh-oh, Timmy needs a new diaper. Mommy is going to put you down right here, okay? Is that okay?" *[Wait.]* "Let's take this wet diaper off, shall we?" *[Wait.]* "Mommy's going to make Timmy all dry and comfy."

I think you get the picture. Use whatever words and phrases you feel comfortable with. The main thing is to keep talking. Talk through the getting up part, the diaper check and change part, the getting dressed part, the carry out of the room part, the going to wherever you're going part. Try to make eye contact whenever possible and don't forget to wait for some kind of response. Acknowledge this response, whatever it is.

Developing a Good Guidance Style

AS FOR MANAGING each of the five important styles that Hart and Risley identified, this is more difficult than just turning up the chat. It will be easier to focus on one style at a time. Set aside some time to play with your baby, preferably when she's on the floor with lots of toys around (lots of choices), and can reach, crawl, or stand to retrieve a toy. Start with the most important style, the one that was found to be the best predictor of a child's verbal ability: guidance style.

The essence of a good guidance style is to be unobtrusive and noncontrolling, while at the same time, encouraging the baby to play with something and engage her in conversation. You don't want your baby to sit passively, staring into space. The controlling mother (or father) wants the baby to play with what she chooses, and if the baby rejects that toy or activity, the mother keeps insisting. Another variation of this type of overcontrol is to remove a toy the child has chosen and substitute one that you prefer: *No, let's play with this one. Mommy wants you to play with this one.*

I once observed a grandmother playing with her grandson who was about two years old. She was the prototypic controlling parent. Everything the child chose to play with was taken away and replaced by something she had chosen. When the child rejected the toy, the grandmother insisted he play with it: *No, we're going to play with this now.* When his rejection was too vigorous, or he was on the verge of tears, the grandmother chose another toy: *Here, play with this instead. Now we're going to play with this. Grandma will show you how this works.* This was done in a domineering tone of voice, and the entire interaction was highly erratic, to the point of interrupting play the grandmother herself had initiated. This continued for the entire time I watched, about thirty minutes. Parents would do well to avoid leaving their child too long with a grandparent (or baby minder) like this. If you discover you have these tendencies, get rid of them quick.

Monitor what you're doing. Tie your mutual play to what *the*

baby has chosen and talk about the toy: *Oh, you've got froggy.*
Show your baby different ways to play with it, making it jump or
hop, and demonstrate how to make it croak. *Look, squeeze his
tummy like this. Listen to the noise froggy makes. Hear him go
croak, croak, croak?* Share toys back and forth. Extend your
hand and ask: *Can Mommy have froggy?* Make froggy hop and
croak, then hand him back. *Here, you make froggy hop.*

If your baby is just sitting there, then offer something. Show
her how a toy works to make it more interesting.

> Look, Mommy can make this wagon go. Can you make
> it go? See, pull this string like this. Watch Mommy do it.
> Now you do it. Good girl! What a clever girl!

Toys don't have to be special. Anything a child can hold or
move that isn't dangerous can be a toy. A universal favorite is a
wooden spoon for banging on a few pans. This is great for learning how to grip objects and move an object relative to another
one to produce a noise. Mutual play can also include joint
movement. If your baby is crawling, then crawl with him; if he
rolls over, you roll over. Babies love it when you imitate them.

Symbolic Emphasis: Making New Connections

SYMBOLIC EMPHASIS MEANS connecting something new to
something the child already knows through analogy, contrast,
similarity, and so forth. This way you can build on the words and
concepts the child understands. For the most part, first words are
names (family and pets), events or routines (things that recur),
and common words that help the child get what he wants or
needs. This is the platform on which you have to build. Don't forget that your child understands far more words than she can say.

You see a man and his dog out for a walk as you push Felicity through the park.

Look, Felicity, that man has a dog. See the man with the brown dog? That dog is big, isn't it? That dog is much bigger than Choy *[the family's Siamese cat]*. Dogs are different from cats. They have different noses and eyes. Do you want to go see the doggie? Shall we ask the man if you can pet his dog? *[Wait for response.]*

Winter is coming. Johnny needs some boots.

We're going to buy you some boots today. Won't that be fun? Do you know what boots are? *[Wait.]* Daddy has some boots. Boots are shoes, but bigger. You'll see when we get to the store. Let's get your coat on and go look at some boots.

Later at the shoe store, John is looking in a mirror.

Look at your feet. One foot has a tall boot, and the other foot has a short shoe. That looks funny, doesn't it? *[Wait.]* Let's put both boots on and see if that looks better. Don't your feet feel snuggly and warm? Boots keep your feet warm when it's cold outside.

Feedback Tone and Language Diversity

I HAVE COMBINED these two styles because they need to be monitored the same way, by taping your interactions with your child. This is especially important if your child isn't reacting to you in a normal, happy way. In this case, tape about half an hour per day of your playtime or mealtime interactions. You are aiming for 100 percent positive comments and zero negative comments. This goal is, of course, impossible to achieve, so settle for around 90 percent positive to 10 percent negative.

Positive feedback sounds like this:

> "Oh what a good girl! Good, you did it! That's a beautiful tower you made." . . . "What a good boy to eat some peas. Look Daddy, Freddie ate four bites of peas and all his meat." . . . "What a nice girl to put your toys in the box. Aren't you helpful." . . . "Well, well, Johnny can chew his meat. What a clever boy. Is it all chewed up now? Aren't you smart."

Negative feedback sounds like this:

> "Watch out, you're going to break that." . . . "No, you can't have that." . . . "No, you can't play with that there." . . . "Put it down now." . . . "You're being a bad girl again." . . . "If you don't eat your peas, you have to get down." . . . "Sit still and stop that. Did you hear what I just said? If you touch that, I'm gonna smack you. Stop wiggling." . . . "You can get down when I say so. Now go to sleep and stop that crying." . . . "What a stupid thing to do, drop your food on the floor. You're being stupid and naughty."

[For parents who never speak like this, these examples seem unreal. I can assure you they are not.]

Parents do need to communicate their important prohibitions, but this doesn't have to involve negative language:

"Oh, sweetie pie, don't touch that, it might fall and break. Mommy will put it up here, so it will be safe." . . . "You mustn't put your fingers in there. That can hurt you and make you cry. Mommy doesn't want you to hurt yourself."

Language diversity refers to a habit of using alternative vocabulary or more complex vocabulary whenever possible. This is harder for parents to judge, because it is specific to the child's current vocabulary and the parents' previous verbal interactions with their infants. Here are some simple examples:

- There is more than one kind of shoe. Take Johnny to the shoe store to buy *boots* or *sandals* or *sneakers*, not just *shoes*.
- Foods have precise names. A mashed banana is *banana*, and not *fruit*.
- There are many different types of juice, such as *orange juice, apple juice, grapefruit juice, cranberry juice*, and not merely *juice*.
- Dogs are distinguished by their size and color: *See the big, black dog*, instead of: *See the dog*.
- *Trains* are not choo-choos. A *van* is different than a *truck* and a *car*.

Responsiveness

RESPONSIVENESS, THE LAST of the five communicative styles, fits closely with guidance style. Responsiveness refers to the ability of parents to follow their child's lead in all reasonable ways, while guidance style means how you talk and how you behave when you're trying to get your child to do something. Responsiveness is being reactive (tuning in), while guidance style is proactive with a positive spin.

In the next chapter, we begin at that magic moment when little Jenny opens her mouth and says (and actually means) her first word.

2.

Getting to Meaning

THE MOST EXCITING PERIOD IN CHILD DEVELOPMENT is the transition from infancy to toddlerhood at around twelve months. Walking, talking, and a myriad of other skills tumble in at the same time. Suddenly, your baby is communicating with you in real words that actually mean something. A personality emerges with full force as Jenny stands up, walks away, waves good-bye, and says *bye-bye* all at once.

Sensory and Motor Milestones

Hearing and Seeing

AT TWELVE MONTHS, basic listening and visual skills are almost as good as an adult's. A one-year-old can hear tones at a much higher pitch than most adults, and he can locate sounds in space reasonably well. He still needs sounds to be louder to hear them as well as you do. Color vision is perfect, and so is vision in depth and stereo-acuity—the ability to see subtle differences in depth. A one-year-old's ability to see fine detail, such as pieces of lint on the furniture, is also good and will get even better over the next few years.

Motor Skills

WALKING

Your toddler will be toddling, or just about to, at around twelve months. She will have practiced standing, struggling around the room clutching onto furniture at about nine or ten months, and stood all by herself with no handholds at eleven or twelve months. But remember, these are averages. Children are different, and not every child fits this timetable. (Children who have spent an hour or two each day in an infant walker tend to be delayed in walking. Contrary to what some parents might think, walkers prevent babies from achieving a sense of balance, and they block babies' view of their feet.)

GRASPING

By now she has mastered the pincer grip, opposing finger and thumb. She can estimate the width or shape of the object she wants to pick up and adjust her hand posture as she is reaching for it. This feat is made possible by her good stereo-acuity. Not only can she pick up objects precisely and smoothly, but she has also just discovered how to unclench her grip. For some reason 'letting go' needs more practice than picking up, and she will practice this new trick with great joy and abandon from any elevated position, the high chair, the stroller, the car seat, wherever dropping something is an option. She will be practicing this for months, because 'controlled release' isn't perfected until about eighteen months of age. Keep in mind that she needs to practice, but be aware that you are at extreme risk. She will rope you into a new game in a heartbeat, called I Drop; You Retrieve. If you don't play your part on cue, you will be punished by loud screams and wails. This game is a backward version of Fetch that people play with their dogs. In your toddler's game, you are assigned the dog's part.

POINTING

Pointing to help another person locate an object in space is a particularly human trait. It requires a complex process of understanding the line of gaze, following the trajectory of the point to an object, and comprehending the mutual aspect of looking—that another person sees the same thing you are looking at. Because of this complexity, pointing has a long developmental path. It starts at around six months when infants begin to look in the same direction mom does. Infants make a point gesture around nine months, which they use in play by themselves. Sometime after this, many infants discover that they can organize mom's entire day by pointing and grunting at everything in sight.

By one year of age all the pieces come together. Toddlers can follow mother's line of sight and her point gesture to the correct place in space. They can point at a distant object and check mom's gaze to see if she is looking in the right direction. At around fifteen months, the toddler is careful to notice whether mom is watching (paying attention) before attempting to point at something in the distance. At the same time, he can use language to get his mom's attention: *Look!* This clearly has become a communicative act: *I want to share what I see with you.*

Language Milestones

First Words

THERE ARE THREE major language milestones between twelve and twenty-four months. The first is the ability to produce words that are intended to mean something, a clear indication that your toddler has both intention and a primitive type of symbolic reasoning:

> I intend to communicate something to you.
> I know that words (vocal noises) represent real objects,
> real persons, and real events in the world.

Baby's first spoken words are drawn from the same repertoire he has been mulling over for the past three months. At last, he says out loud a few of the words that he knows. These first words must meet two criteria: They are the most important words *for him* for this communication in this context, and they are the easiest for him to produce.

The latest research shows that first words are more often about events than anything else. Next comes names for persons, animals, and even fuzzy toys. Words for objects are last on the list. But toddlers vary in what interests them, and each child will have his or her unique set of first words. Following is a table listing some of the common first words that toddlers say. Be aware that she won't be saying all of these words, only a few of them. Nor will your toddler's words sound like they are written here. *Juice*, a favorite word, will sound more like *doo* or *doose*.

Once babbling is well underway, and especially when first words come in, exaggerated Motherese starts to disappear. The

First Words

BABIES' FIRST WORDS could come from anywhere on this list. Each baby is different, and each baby will say the words that are the most important to him. Remember, it's perfectly normal for a baby's first word to appear as early as ten months and as late as two years. And keep in mind that few of these first words will be pronounced correctly.

EVENT WORDS: bath, breakfast, lunch, dinner, bed, sleep, walk, wash, play, go home

PERSONS: mommy, daddy, baby, granny, grandpa, Teddy, dolly; *names of:* siblings, family pet, fuzzy toys, dollies

BODY PARTS: belly button, nose, ear, mouth, eye, hand, toe, finger, hair, arm, leg

CLOTHES: shoe, pajamas, hat, dress, sock, pants, shirt

FOOD: juice, apple, cheese, cookie, cereal, milk, cracker

ANIMALS: doggie, kitty, bunny, duck, puppy, horse, bird, fish

OBJECTS: car, toys, truck, dolly, blocks, cup, dish, bowl, bed, chair, a bath toy (boat, duck), blanket, potty, and any *particular toy*

DESCRIPTION WORDS: big, little, nice, bad, good, pretty, soft, hard, yummy, yucky, sad, mad, red, yellow, green, blue, black, white

ACTION VERBS: eat, drink, walk, run, clap, stand, sit, come, go, play, sleep, wash, drop, pick-it-up, kiss, hug, see, look, get, get-up, get-down, take, give

NONACTION VERBS: have, want, like, love, have, am, is, was

SOCIAL WORDS: hi, hello, bye-bye, please, thank you, good night (nite-nite)

ABSTRACT: no, yes, out, in, home, whutsat? gone, all-gone, that, there, uh-oh, me, my pitch of your voice drops. Modulations are less extreme. Instead, mothers speak in what is called 'infant-directed speech.' Phrases are simple and short, as before, but now mother expands on baby's new word. The baby who utters a clear *doose* while reaching for a cup of juice, is likely to hear back: *Yes, that's your juice. It's apple juice. You like juice, don't you? Mommy likes juice too. Juice is good.*

Infant-directed speech continues until well beyond the second year. Research on children aged eighteen to twenty-four months showed that they *only* learned a new word in a training session when they heard it in infant-directed speech, and did not learn it when they heard it in adult-directed speech, such as in conversations between mom and dad—more evidence to underscore the importance of parent-infant conversations.

Something else happens when first words start appearing. A magic genie pulls a switch in your brain and you become an instant sportscaster. If you watch yourself, you'll notice that you are producing running commentaries on what your toddler is doing. This monologue is produced in crisp, well-articulated phrases.

> Oh, you're going to put that toy in the box. Uh-oh,
> you dropped it. Are you going to pick it up? Okay,
> you're not. John's got his big racing car. That's a
> big car. You can make it go round and round. Very
> good. That's very fast, isn't it?

Of course your toddler doesn't need this monologue to inform him about his actions. He knows perfectly well what he's doing. The question is, does he need it to help develop his language skills? And if he does need it, why did mom wait until now to talk this way? So far, we have no answers to these questions. It seems obvious that mom's speaking style must have something to do with helping her toddler put his actions into words. If mom's sportscaster mode of speaking follows the pattern of the research results so far, then *mother knows best* when it comes to speaking in the most appropriate manner for her child.

During the first half of the second year, the toddler's spoken words appear rather slowly, at around eight to twelve words a month. They are produced with great seriousness and even visible effort. Sometimes you can watch the wheels turn as the toddler searches for a word, then works out how to make it, and finally utters it. When my son was thirteen months old, we moved to a new house. For a week, he was miserable, whining, fussing, looking up with that expression of unbearable pain and suffering that only toddlers can muster. This misery persisted despite everyone else's obvious happiness with the new house, the family being intact, plus the same furniture, the same toys, the same bed and bedtime companions: doggy, bunny, Pooh. I asked him repeatedly what was wrong, but he only whined in mute suffering.

After five days, he purposefully got my attention, walked me to the front door, and reached up on tiptoe to touch the doorknob. Then he said in crystal clear tones, *Go home now Mommy*. The mime, followed by a grammatically accurate, four-word sentence was wrenched from the depths of despair, the effort to compose it lasting several days. Of course, once we understood what was bothering him, we could easily fix it. We explained, *This is our new home. This is our new home now*. As he understood *new*, *home*, and *now*, and obviously could grasp word order sufficiently to utter a grammatically correct sentence, he was satisfied with this information. It was the strangeness he wanted explained and the *duration* of the strangeness (the uncertainty), hence his use of a time marker, *now*.

The Vocabulary Explosion

AFTER THE TODDLER has spent many months mastering the early phase of speech production, there is an abrupt shift in the number of new words she begins to produce each day. This is known as 'the vocabulary explosion.' There are two estimates for the onset of the vocabulary explosion. The first is *age*—sometime around eighteen months. The second is the *number of words* in the toddler's spoken vocabulary. The explosion starts after the first 50 or so words appear. The estimate based on vocabulary size is more accurate than the estimate based on age.

Keep a record of your baby's new words to track this new developmental milestone. If it's too late to begin at the beginning, or you haven't kept a diary, jot down how many words he or she is using now. When there are around 50 on the list, new words should start tumbling out faster than you can keep up with them. It has been estimated that across the age range from two to six years, children must be learning about 8 to 10 new words per day to achieve the vocabulary they have at age six. The current estimate of a typical six-year-old's receptive vocabulary (words they understand but may not say) is around 13,000 words.

Your Toddler's Language Style

ABOUT THIRTY YEARS AGO, Katherine Nelson discovered that children's first words tend to fall into one of two categories. She studied speech production at the 50-word stage, and found that, for some children, 75 percent of their vocabulary consisted of referential nouns, words that *refer* directly to something in the environment: events, people, animals, food. Other children used a greater variety of word types and far fewer referential nouns (only 34 percent of their vocabulary). She interpreted these contrasting styles as "referential" and "expressive," noting more social words for the latter group like *thank you, please, bye-bye, good night, hello, okay.* These categories did not hold up in subsequent research, though there was support for Nelson's referential type, children who use mainly single, common nouns in the early phases of speech production. But nonreferential children weren't necessarily more expressive. Instead, these children were more likely to use short word strings or mini phrases.

Elena Lieven recorded children's speech at frequent intervals from just before they entered the 50-word stage to just after the 100-word stage. Mothers' diaries were also used to compile each child's spoken vocabulary. This was sorted into single words and multiword phrases, then categorized by parts of speech. Two main types of utterance accounted for over 50 percent of all utterances: *common nouns* and *'frozen phrases.'* A frozen phrase is defined as a phrase that springs into being as a whole; that is, none of the individual words has previously been produced in isolation. Lieven's examples include: *all-gone, oh-dear, where's-it-gone, there-it-is.*

There was compelling evidence for two distinct styles of language development, because these two types of utterance were strongly, *negatively* correlated—the more single words the child used, the fewer the frozen phrases, and vice versa, and this pattern grew stronger over time (from the first 50 words to 100 words). For readers familiar with statistics, the correlation at the 50-word level was -0.72, and at the 100-word level, -0.84 (a perfect correlation is 1.0).

Equally important, Lieven found that children do not mistake a frozen phrase for a single, long word. Instead, they use these phrases to construct new ones by swapping the words in and out, rather like variations on a theme: *All-gone* can become *Mommy-gone*, *bye-bye-gone*, *yum-yum-gone*. This shows that children are very clear about what a word is and what a phrase is.

Lieven believes that this reflects two distinct modes of language acquisition. One type of child builds language from the bottom up, word by word, eventually putting words together, rather like building a house with bricks. The other type of child builds language by phrases from the outset, constructing other phrases and sentences by swapping the words in and out, rather like building a house with modules.

Although the number of children in this study was small, there was a striking sex difference. On average, the boys produced isolated common nouns at about three times the rate of frozen phrases, and *no boy produced more frozen phrases than nouns*. Half of the girls followed suit, but the other half produced three times as many frozen phrases as common nouns. The age of the child was not a factor and had no bearing on the style the child used. Nor was there any connection to *speed* of language acquisition. Boys and girls had the same vocabulary size, and took the same amount of time (two months) to get from 50 to 100 words of spoken vocabulary.

So far, we don't know how or whether these two styles of language acquisition affect subsequent language development. And even if we did know, there would be no way for parents to influence which style their child adopted. Nevertheless, these patterns are extremely intriguing, and it would be interesting for parents to pay attention and find out which kind of child they have.

The vocabulary expansion, or explosion, isn't so much a stage of word acquisition, like a brain module switching on, as it is an indication of how much time infants need to practice making words. In essence, a sudden flood of spoken words marks the end of a 'block' in speech production. The toddler spends the first half of his second year focusing so intently on how to produce speech that he doesn't have much attention left over when he tries to talk. Once he has reached a critical level of speaking skill, he can look around and enjoy the roses. Words stored in memory start tumbling out.

Suddenly toddlers can monitor various social cues *while they are talking*, something they couldn't do before. They can express emotion and speak at the same time. The earnestness is gone, and the toddler can smile with one word, frown with another, and look sad with another. This is a clear example of what happens when something difficult becomes practiced, and less effort is needed to do it. It's like driving a car for the first time versus driving a car a year later. Once something starts to become automatic, it doesn't need all your attention, and you can do several things at once. A toddler can move, smile, and say a word, all at the same time. Just as you can drive, listen to your passenger, drink coffee, and notice traffic lights all at the same time. This juggling act is called parallel processing, something that humans and animals become expert at, but so far computers have not.

Two-Word Sentences

THE THIRD MILESTONE follows almost immediately after the vocabulary explosion. This is known as the two-word sentence phase, which starts around eighteen to twenty months. However, this phase may need to be modified in view of Lieven's discoveries. The referential child, who produces mainly common nouns, goes through the two-word phase, but the child who builds language mainly from frozen phrases is there from the start. In either case, two-word sentences are usually grammatically correct, in that the word order is correct.

Typical two-word sentences are: *come Mommy, big dog, blue dress, kiss Daddy, feed kitty, have bath, tie shoe,* and so forth. Of course, pronunciation won't be this precise. Toddlers have particular trouble with adjacent consonants. So *blue dress* is likely to come out *boo dess,* then later *blue dwess.* Getting this right can take several years. Speech accuracy continues to improve well into the teens. So if your youngster struggles with certain speech patterns for a long, long time, this is not cause for alarm.

Parents whose children have serious language delays, that is, no speech or little speech according to these milestones, should seek the advice of their pediatrician. Assuming that hearing is normal, a child with extreme delays in spoken language (less than 10 words at eighteen to twenty months) should be tested. He should be given tests for speech-motor problems, and a test of *receptive* vocabulary. It is very important to know how much he understands of what people say. I'll say more about late talkers in Chapter 3, but I will say now that it is impossible to predict whether a late talker will suddenly blossom until he or she is around the age of five.

What Do Babies Really Know?

BABY BOOKS, pediatricians, and even some researchers, estimate language development according to how many words infants or toddlers can *say.* Your pediatrician's guidelines for language development are based on the words in the average child's spoken vocabulary. We have already seen that infants at the babbling stage can understand scores of words and can't say any of them. Nothing changes in this regard as the baby grows older, and perhaps at no time in childhood is there such a discrepancy between understanding speech and producing it than during the second year of life. Children understand about four times as many words as they can say. The language milestones I have described so far are milestones of speech production, not what the toddler actually understands. We've just reached the two-word sentence milestone. Does this mean that toddlers understand only two words in every sentence? Roberta Golinkoff and Kathy Hirsh-Pasek decided to find out.

They asked toddlers questions by showing them two videos on two TV screens at the same time. The baby sat on his mother's lap facing a blank space between the screens. He had to turn his head to look at a video, and how long he looked at each video was timed. The babies were given a little quiz. If they knew the right answer they studied one of the videos much longer than the other. Here is one of the simpler problems the babies were asked to solve. Could they tell the difference between two sentences in which the same action (kissing) was directed to one of two different objects (keys or a ball)? In each video the same woman kissed an object (keys or a ball) and the 'unkissed' object dangled in her other hand. They asked the babies, "Where is the lady kissing the ball?" or "Where is the lady kissing the keys?" Even thirteen- to fifteen-month-old babies had no trouble with this one, and always looked at the right video. They understood not only the words, but also the action-object relationship in a sentence.

Next, they tried something harder. Can toddlers follow word order in a sentence? In English, we can say, "John jumped over the fence and ran," but not "Jumped ran over John the fence and." English has a word order grammar. Different languages have different types of grammatical structure, and babies must solve different grammar problems depending on the language they have to learn. When do babies begin to solve the agent-action-object word order problem?

Sitting in front of two video screens, toddlers heard either: "Cookie Monster is tickling Big Bird" or "Big Bird is tickling Cookie Monster." The thirteen- to fifteen-month-olds failed this task, looking equally often at both videos. But by sixteen to eighteen months, babies knew exactly who was tickling whom. They used the word order in a sentence to figure out who was the actor who was acted upon.

When infants utter two-word sentences, they obviously choose the most important words to get the message across. But is this because they can't *say* all the words in the sentence, or because they can't *remember* the words long enough to say them, or because they don't *pay attention* to unimportant words? For years everyone thought the last answer was true, especially for function words, those little words like *a, the, if, with*. It didn't seem likely that toddlers would notice these insignificant, abstract words.

The research team showed a picture-book to eighteen- to twenty-month-old children. Each page had four pictures. The child's job was to find the right picture. He was asked to do this in one of four different ways. Each way was designed to find out what he knew about the word *the* and whether this word was important in a sentence:

> Find the dog for me. *[The conventional way]*
> Find dog for me. *[Okay but missing the]*
> Find was dog for me. *[Confusing because* was *is sitting
>   where* the *is supposed to go, and* was *is not where it
>   normally goes in a sentence.]*
> Find gub dog for me. *[Confusing because* gub *isn't a
>   word the child has heard before.]*

If toddlers ignore little words like *the*, they had all the information they needed in every sentence to find the dog. How did they do on this task? They scored a whopping 86 percent correct when they heard the first type of sentence, and 75 percent correct when they heard the second. These are both excellent scores, but clearly, the word *the* did help a lot. When *was* (the third sentence) was substituted, this was very disruptive, and the average score plummeted to 56 percent correct. They did even worse when they were thrown by a new word (*gub*) sitting in front of *dog*. Now we have a new type of sentence. *Gub* could be an adjective, and its position in the sentence directs them to find a *gub dog*, a type of dog. The toddlers were baffled, and scored only 36 percent correct, no better than guessing.

It's clear that toddlers pay close attention to every word in the sentence. Otherwise they couldn't work out how words modify each other and change meaning. But what about the *pieces* of words that change meaning, like verb endings or adverb endings? Surely toddlers wouldn't notice the difference between the present participle (slow*ing*) and its adverb form (slow*ly*). Eighteen- to twenty-month-old toddlers were shown two videos at the same time. First they heard "Where's the dancing?" No problem. They looked at the video where people were dancing. Then they heard "Where's the dancely?" Babies got confused. Scores dipped dramatically for a few tries. Then suddenly the babies seemed to get it: *Hmm, I guess dancely means the same as dancing in this game.* But when they heard "Where's the danceloo?" they were completely stumped. *Loo* isn't a word ending in English. Maybe a *danceloo* is a new kind of thing or person or creature.

I hope you're suitably impressed with your toddler's ability to understand speech, but now that I've let you in on the secret world of the toddler, you need to beware. Think twice about those casual remarks at breakfast and dinner. Don't imagine that your toddler doesn't understand. Your toddler is spying on you. She understands way more than you think she does.

How Toddlers Communicate Without Language

While your toddler is struggling to produce her first words, she will be communicating with you in other ways.

Imitation: Insight into Self and Other

IT'S A FACT THAT INFANTS, children, and adults imitate others. Like our primate ancestors, 'monkey see, monkey do.' This can be seen in the game of Peekaboo, which mothers initiate quite early. Mom hides her face or head (or the baby's) with a cloth, then pulls away the cloth and says *peekaboo*. Up to one year of age, baby watches and squeals in delight. But at one year, she begins to take turns playing this game, something she will do over and over again. Now she grabs the cloth, drapes it over her head, snatches it away, squeals and maybe utters *boo*. The baby has created a game format of conversational turn-taking, *communicating about shared intentions*. This is definitely something that monkeys don't do.

Andrew Meltzoff did this experiment to test infants' memories. (Meltzoff also did the study cited earlier on newborns' ability to imitate facial gestures, such as sticking out your tongue.) Toddlers, twelve months old, were brought into the laboratory. They were seated on their mother's lap and witnessed a strange event. A person walked in, bent over, and touched the lid of a box with his forehead, and the box lit up. Then the stranger departed. Later, the baby was brought back and seated in such a way that she could touch her head to the box that was sitting in front of her. Most of the babies could remember this incident and imitated this gesture after a delay of one week. (So much for the theory that babies can't remember anything.) The older the child, the longer the memory stayed in mind. By eighteen months, children could remember and imitate this behavior after a four-month delay!

The same effect can be demonstrated in reverse. A group of mothers and their toddlers were brought into a playroom with lots of toys on a table, two of each kind. Half the mothers stood opposite their toddlers and imitated everything they did. The other mothers and toddlers played with the different toys. At around fourteen months, the babies caught on. The toddlers who were being imitated looked and smiled at their mothers much more often than the other toddlers did, and then tried to test them out, watching to see what they would do. At this age the toddler knows he is a separate self interacting with another separate self.

Toddlers understand they are separate from other people. But *how* separate, and *how deep* does this perception go? You might want to try this experiment designed by Alison Gopnik and Betty Rapacholi. Put your child in a chair at a table and place two bowls in front of him. One should contain some type of cracker the baby likes (Goldfish crackers, animal crackers). The other should contain pieces of raw broccoli. Ask your toddler if he wants to try some. (They never take the broccoli.) Now *you* taste the food in the bowls. When you eat the broccoli, smile and say, *Yummy*, or whatever you normally say. When you eat the crackers make a face like they're disgusting, and say something like *Yucky*. After a minute or two, push the two bowls closer to your child, hold out your hand and ask, "*Can you give Mommy some?*" Toddlers younger than about eighteen months will give you the crackers *because they like them*, even though they saw that you didn't. Sometime between eighteen and twenty-four months they will give you the broccoli *even though they don't like it*. Now your child can take someone else's perspective and act in a way that benefits the other person, even when this contradicts his own intentions and desires. This is quite a magical transformation. [If you think your child already knows too much about your tastes in food, try the same experiment with a familiar neighbor or friend as a substitute for you.]

Pretend Play

TODDLERS NOT ONLY BEGIN to understand self and other, but also what is real and unreal, which they show in pretend play. One-year-olds happily pretend that they are carrying out a real event in the wrong context. Sometimes they do this as a joke, smiling or giggling while it is going on. These pretend games often involve a well-known routine. Billy will pretend to take a bath on the living room floor with pretend soap (maybe a piece of a puzzle). Andrea will get a blanket or cloth, carefully drape it on the floor, curl up on top and close her eyes. Then she'll peek up at you to see if you're enjoying the joke, and laugh. Sam enjoys a chat on an imaginary telephone, and he enjoys this even more when mom talks back on another imaginary telephone. Toddlers do not confuse real events with these pretend events. They know they are acting in a play of their own construction.

Toddlers co-opt toys into their fantasy play as well. Toys are used as stand-ins for people and things. A banana might be a telephone. A doll can be held aloft and fly around the room like a bird. A block can be a car (*vroom-vroom*). As your child grows older, play can involve some quite sophisticated thinking, and what your child does is very revealing about what he knows. For example, Tommy is playing with blocks, trying to build a tower that doesn't fall down. He adds two spectators to watch the tower going up. First, he sets aside a big block and says,

Mommy, then a little block and says, *Tommy*. Not only has he demonstrated that he understands relative size (big, little), but he has also *generalized* relative size to inanimate objects as a concept. This is quite a leap.

As your toddler gets older, games get more intricate, more and more fanciful, and sillier. The toddler's sense of humor, I'm afraid, is just about as silly as it gets. Your main line of defense is to join in. You can find out some interesting things this way. Sit with your child on the floor while he is playing with his toys. Ask silly questions with a serious expression, pretending that you don't really know the answers to such profound questions: Does a block have a bath? Does a block eat lunch? Do cars take naps? Put some toys under a little blanket, including fuzzy toys like Teddy, and ask which one takes a nap. Does Teddy have lunch? Have you seen him chew? Which toy can talk? You'll be surprised by the reactions you get. You'll see clearly where reality ends and unreality begins, and it's not always where you might imagine. (Teddies definitely take a nap, need their sleep, but as to needing food??? well this will take some thought—nobody ever sees them eating.)

You can see the flowering of imagination in these examples, something that word counts and word types don't capture at all. Word counts give the impression that toddlers collect words in the same way you would collect pretty shells on a beach. In this type of model, when a toddler hears a word about something that interests him, he files it in a mental file drawer so he can find it again. He collects words in the same way a lepidopterist collects butterflies, carefully pinning them in place in his mind. In this view, words are simply tokens, a set of vocal patterns that get you what you want and help you share some concerns, and that's about it. But this doesn't tell us anything about the world the toddler lives in. It doesn't shed any light on the kinds of problems your toddler is trying to solve, or what is really going on in his mind.

The Really Deep Questions

Imagine yourself on Crypton, a distant planet, where you have been transported by alien abductors. You are a captive of strange creatures who have taken you in a spaceship to live in their world. You are surrounded by Cryptonians who jabber constantly in shrill, unintelligible noises. A Crypton minder is assigned to you, and its job is to move you back and forth from room A to room B. Things happen in room A that do not happen in room B, and these things tend to repeat in some kind of pattern or sequence. They are unfamiliar and so seem utterly meaningless.

Each day at a particular time, you are taken to room C and participate in some kind of joint activity. In room C, several Cryptonians meet and form into a circle. In the middle of the circle is a big pile of something green. All the Cryptonians take pieces from the pile. They don't use hands, because their "hands" are more like a pair of elephant trunks. Then they rub the green pieces around on their knobbly bodies. They nudge you with these trunks in an effort to make you join in, and you do, imitating them. They seem to enjoy this activity, because, as time goes by, they make more and more soft gurgling noises, instead of the sharp, loud noises they make the rest of the time. When this ritual ends, the Cryptonians go away and you are taken to room B. An arm/trunk waves you to lie down on the floor. By now it's dark. You fall asleep, and the whole thing starts over the next day. [I should point out that you might not live very long on Crypton, because Cryptonians take in food through pores on their bodies, and you don't.]

Think about what would be uppermost in your mind in this

situation (assuming you aren't really going to die). If you have a good imagination, you won't have any trouble thinking of scores of questions you would like to answer. When you have tried to answer the most important ones, you'll have a fair idea of how an infant thinks from about nine months until the end of the second year of life.

First of all, you would ask: "Am I safe? Are these Cryptonians going to harm me? Can I trust this particular Cryptonian who has been assigned to move me from room to room?" By *trust* you also mean predictability. Is what happens predictable so I can stop being surprised? When things are predictable, one event will follow another in time in a sequence or chain. *Predictable* means that what is in room A stays the same, and what is in room B stays the same. It means that how long you stay in a particular room and what you do in it is the same day after day (the Cryptonian day of course, which by our clock is forty-six hours long). We call the predictability within and between different contexts, at specific times of day, taking specific amounts of time, routines. Fixed routines are comforting; the mind can focus on other things.

Then you notice that some events always seem to follow as a consequence of a preceding event. For example, you observe a group of Cryptonians on a hillside tossing some of the green stuff into the air. It rises up and up until it disappears completely. You notice that the Cryptonians seem to get happy when they rub the green stuff on their bodies. You ask yourself, did the throwing *cause* the stuff to disappear? Is there something very odd about the nature of gravity on Crypton that can *cause* the green stuff to escape into outer space? Did the green stuff *make* the Cryptonians happy? A situation where one event follows as a consequence of another is called causality.

Then there are those noises the Cryptonians make. Do they mean anything? Perhaps if you listen carefully and can discover when and where *particular* noises are used, you might be able to predict better what is going on. Maybe you can begin to understand how to get through to them, find out what interests them, and why they do things. Maybe you can signal your urgent desire to return to Earth.

These kinds of questions arise in the mind of someone who can consciously reflect on her own thoughts. But they are no different from the kinds of questions that infants must tackle without the benefit of self-conscious reflection (aware of being aware), language, or previous experience to compare it to. Infants *do* have the benefit of evolution, which you do not on Crypton. They belong in the environment they were born into, and they come equipped with some inborn talents that will eventually help them answer all the questions you struggled with on Crypton.

Understanding predictability by being able to isolate routines from whatever else is going on, and noticing what causes what, are both problems of *mastering time*. Time is not real, not an absolute. It is not something provided by a time module in the brain. Time must be extracted from experience.

How Do Toddlers Master Time?

It's mom's job to structure her toddler's day, and she does so with predictable routines and time words. Parents are time-minders by profession. Time words accompany activities from the infant's earliest days, when mom chattered about anything and everything to a semi-alert creature who couldn't understand a word. But as soon as it becomes obvious that your infant understands something you are saying, time words are frequent markers in many interactions. Toddlers may not use many time words until after age two, but they certainly understand that time words mark something about event sequences long before then.

The first concept of time a toddler can grasp is the 'now' and 'not-now.' The 'time world' usually begins around eighteen months of age. In the now/not-now time world, there is the immediate present, and everything that is not the immediate present (past or future, makes no difference). Mom marks this constantly as the day wears on in statements like: "Now we're going to have our lunch. Now we need to take a bath. Now help Mommy pick up the toys. Right now, you will have to wait" (a contradiction for a toddler). And moms say to whiny toddlers who are pointing to the cookie jar, "*Not now.*" In the story about my toddler who said, "*Go home* now *Mommy,*" he was trying to say that he wanted his presence in that strange house to become *not now.*

During the period between eighteen and twenty-four months, toddlers will store away a vocabulary of time words that they will try hard to understand but seldom produce. These words fit into a broad group of time categories:

> **location in time:** *now, not now, when, soon, later, in a minute, already, bedtime, lunchtime, come on (meaning "now"), morning, night, afternoon, evening, tomorrow, yesterday*
>
> **sequence in time:** *and then, while, first, before, next, after, so, since, when, yet*
>
> **duration in time:** *wait, until, long, short, little while, still, over, stay, forever*
>
> **frequency in time:** *always, never, sometimes, maybe, again, next time*
>
> **speed:** *fast, slow, quick, hurry, dawdle*

Parents are also careful to provide verbal time boundaries as start and stop markers for various events and episodes:

Let's play. Let's go. Let's have a —. Time for lunch. We're all done. We're finished. That's enough. We have to stop. Don't start that. That's the end. It's all over. It's all gone.

Unlike the subtlety and richness of time words for markers and routines, causality gets short shrift in English:

causality: *because, cause, if-then*

The concept of causality is highly abstract (the reason for this is that), and toddlers find it difficult to fit causality words into their speech, even though they understand certain aspects of causality perfectly. Witness the twelve-month-olds who imitated the man who touched his head to a box, which *caused* it to light up, *even after one week had gone by.*

We use time words so often that it comes as a surprise to realize these are actually time words. Adults are much more likely to think of time in terms of clock time or historical time. Young children don't reach this level of understanding until they go to school, and then they must be carefully taught. Clock time and historical time are not where infants, toddlers, or preschoolers *live*. Nor would clock time be where you lived if you had been abducted to Crypton, and they took away your watch.

How Do Toddlers Represent Time in Language?

ROUTINES

During the first two years of life, the child has to sort out some major puzzles. First he must learn about routines by participating in them. Then he has to grasp their logical structure in some form or other. Until he does this, he can't represent action sequences accurately with language.

Simple routines are AND structures, which work by addition: one event + another + another. a + b + c + d + e. To represent this structure in language, all you need is the word *and*, or better still, *and then*. But this is merely a description of the structure itself, and tells us nothing about the subtleties or complexities of time within the structure, such as:

> *I take a bath each* **evening,** after *I watch my*
> *favorite TV show, but* **before** *Dad gets home from*
> **night** *shift. I have to* **hurry,** *because it takes a* **long**
> **time** *for the water to heat up* **again.**

In Toddlerese, a description of a routine takes the basic form:

> *We go upstairs,* **and** *we run the water,* **and** *I take*
> *off my clothes,* **and** *I get in the tub,* **and** *Mommy*
> *puts soap on me,* **and** *Mommy washes it off,* **and** *I*
> *get out,* **and** *I get a towel,* **and** *I get all dry.*

This is the toddler's full bath scenario, assuming he can string all these phrases together, which he can't. If you ask a toddler, "What's a bath?" he would be more likely to say:

> *My up, Timmy ba-ba.*

It will be a while before he makes it clear these two events are connected:

> *My, me, mommy go up* **and** *Timmy bath.*

Sometime between two and three years, we get the more sophisticated version:

> *I go upstairs* **and then** *I take a bath.*

Also, sometime after twenty-four months, the child starts experimenting with time words, often used incorrectly:

> **Somenight** *I go upstairs, and* **in a minute** *I get a bath.*

Which means, or might mean:

> **Every night** *I go upstairs, and Mom says,*
> *"I'll run your bath* **in a minute."**

The child has muddled *sometime* and *somenight*. He uses the wrong word, but in the right slot in the sentence. He doesn't know that *in a minute* can't stand alone without a person saying it.

The following example shows how long it takes to get this sorted out. Here's a thirty-five-month-old boy's response to the request *Tell me a story*. He doesn't have much imagination for storytelling, but he does have the morning routine worked out, even if the order of events is completely scrambled:

> *The daddy works in the bank* and *Mommy cooks break-fast*. Then *we get up* and *get dressed*. And *the baby eats breakfast* and *honey*. *We go to the school* and *we get dressed like that*. *I put coat on* and *I go in the car*.
> (Applebee 1978, p. 59)

[All of a sudden, this child changed topic and began talking about bears and lions, as if he realized this 'story' was becoming incredibly boring.]

CAUSE AND EFFECT

Framing the logic of causality in order to represent it in language is fiendishly difficult. It is an IF-THEN structure, which requires a coupling of two events in which one event is the consequence of the other. Despite the difficulties in framing this logic in words, infants have no problem whatsoever in perceiving direct causality in the physical world.

In one experiment, toddlers were tested to see if they could follow a causal chain, and tell it apart from a broken chain:

> A causes B, which in turn causes C.
> A causes B. B causes C.

On the face of it, this sounds like an extremely difficult problem. The toddlers were shown two versions of a cartoon video in which two vehicles were featured. The scientists used a complex procedure to measure which vehicle the infant watched and when. This allowed them to discover how the infant perceived the two events.

Event 1. Toy vehicle 1 smashes into toy vehicle 2, which in turn smashes into a house, at which point a puppy pops out. There is no delay between the time the first vehicle hits the second vehicle and when it starts moving toward the house. A → B → C

Event 2. Everything is the same, except after vehicle 1 smashes into vehicle 2, vehicle 2 doesn't move for two seconds. Then it starts moving and smashes into the house. A → B. B → C

The results showed that fifteen-month-old toddlers can tell the difference between these two events, because they focus most attention on the vehicle that *really caused* the house to be hit and the puppy to pop out. Solving this problem hinges on noticing the difference between a zero delay and a two-second delay.

The brains of humans and animals are hard-wired to be sensitive to co-occurrences, coincidences, and sequences of events in the world. This is one reason why humans are so superstitious. And this is why the toddlers could solve the causality problem in the experiment. But events occurring in immediate time (right before your eyes) is only one kind of causality. There is another, deeper, type of causality, where the connection between events isn't at all obvious. We call this type of causality 'reasons.'

Unfortunately, English uses the same connector word for both types of causality. If you call your husband on the phone and say, "We can't get in *because* I locked the key in the house," there is no connection in time between these two phrases. You might have locked in your house keys hours before, gone to the mall and the supermarket, chatted with your neighbor over the fence, and then tried to open your door. But in the sentence "You fell over because you tripped on that rock," the connection is immediate and obvious.

Toddlers have trouble understanding causality words, and they have equal trouble using them in their own speech. The best you're likely to get before the end of the second year is two phrases in a sequence, possibly with *and* in the middle. Notice that this is the same construction toddlers use for routines that have no causality. (Going upstairs does not *cause you* to have a bath.) So toddlers will say, *Teddy fall. Teddy cry,* or *Teddy fall* AND *Teddy cry*, meaning, *Falling* CAUSED *Teddy to cry*. When children are two or older they might use *and then* to imply that Teddy cried as a consequence of falling, but this is still ambiguous. It could be a coincidence: *Teddy fall* AND THEN *Teddy cry*.

As you can see, it is a formidable problem to express what you know about reasons and causes. The English language actually conspires against the child, because the temporal order is reversed so that the *effect precedes the cause* in a sentence. There's the added problem that causality words are 'connectors' that sit in a slot between two sentences or phrases.

> Grandma is in the hospital because she fell down and broke her leg.

> The dog is hungry because nobody fed him last night.

Toddlers have difficulty mastering one sentence, much less joining up two sentences in reverse temporal order. All these problems must be solved before a toddler can understand and say even this simple sentence: *Teddy cry* 'CAUSE *Teddy fall down.*

When children reach the *why* stage, they are earnestly seeking reasons. Parents have a big job trying to explain reasons to their young children, and trying to get them to expand on what they really mean. There is a way to help. First, turn time the right way around so that the cause precedes the effect. English allows you to do this. It just takes a few more words. In the grandma situation, a parent could say:

> Grandma fell down and hurt herself and that is why Grandma is in the hospital now.

Now repeat this information with the phrases reversed so the child can hear what *because* means:

> You see, grandma is in the hospital **because** she fell down.

Then expand it.

A hospital is where people go when they get hurt.
The hospital can help Grandma get all well.

Young children try very hard to understand what's going on, just as you did on Crypton. If they don't understand causes and reasons about something they feel is important, they can get quite confused and even distressed, though they might not show it. Parents always do their best to explain everything they can, but parents need to know that causal language doesn't always help. Adults use '*because*' almost as second nature. To a toddler it has no meaning, especially for making connections between events separated in time, or events that are related in complex ways.

PAST, PRESENT, AND FUTURE TIME

Here's another situation that can be misleading for parents. Our grammar marks past, present, and future tense in every sentence. These tense markers appear in the speech of a toddler long before he has much idea about the nature of past time, present time, and future time. Yet by the end of the second year, many children are using the present participle (the immediate now— go*ing*, runn*ing*), past tense, and future tense verbs with some skill. So we know they understand something new about time. What has been added is a new twist to the now/not-now world. Toddlers have worked out that there is a difference between events that *precede* 'now' and those that *follow* 'now.' This is not the same as saying that toddlers have any real understanding of past and future, time, or of time extension. It just means that toddlers have three baskets instead of two for sorting time:

1. now
2. the thing that happened that I remember, but it isn't 'now'

3. the thing that Dad is telling me about that hasn't happened yet, but isn't 'now'

It will take many years and many different kinds of experiences before a child really understands the difference between time-span words for clock time and historical time like: *ten minutes, an hour, one day, last week, next year, when you were little, wait until Christmas.*

Words Without Communication

SO FAR, WE HAVE SEEN that infants and toddlers have been working hard to try to communicate with their parents and other people in the household. It is always the intent of the communication that drives the interactions, finally producing, at twelve months or so, a few words that mean what the baby wants to say or comment about. He has been carefully picking these words, because he is particularly interested in these persons, events, and objects. Trying to say what you mean, and talk about what interests you, is what language is for. But late in the second year, something new happens. The toddler starts using words that have no meaning *for him*. Because the new words appear in the correct sequence in a sentence and are spoken fluently, parents often mistakenly believe the child means the same thing they do by these words.

Katherine Nelson calls this "use before meaning." Nelson studied this, among other things, by recording a toddler's bedtime conversations with her father, and then when she was left alone. When Emily was tucked in for the night, and dad left the room, she talked herself to sleep. Young children's monologues are quite common, and parents would do well to eavesdrop. The recordings began when Emily was twenty-one months old and lasted until she was three years old. I have chosen one example because it is also relevant to the issue of causality.

Dad, like most parents, uses *because* and *'cause* constantly to answer most of Emily's questions and explain why grandma can't come/didn't come, why Emily has to go to sleep now, why she has to go to sleep at all, why she can't have another drink, why she can't have anything more to eat, etc.

Here are three quotes from dad:

> Everyone is going to sleep *because*
>   you know what happens in the nighttime?
> Everybody's asleep *'cause* it's— *[interrupted]*
> Be quick about it *because* we have to go to sleep.
>   (Nelson 1998, p. 141)

In Emily's monologues she often rehearsed phrases she heard her father say. If dad used *because* a lot, so did she, but not in any meaning dad intended. It appeared in specific contexts (sleep) that dad had used, but made no sense. The following quotes are from Emily at twenty-one months:

> *Emmy went to sleep 'cause Mor.* [her name for grandma]
> *Emmy didn't go to sleep 'cause in bed.*
> *Emmy went to sleep 'cause Mommy, Mormor* [grandma]
> *Emmy get up.* (p. 142)

Notice that Emily has the word *'cause* exactly where it should be in the sentence, as a connector at the end of the first clause. What she can't do is provide a second clause much less connect the clauses logically. Emily seems to be exercising her grammar muscle, not her logic muscle.

At twenty-eight months she appears to have more success:

> *We'll have to go in the green car 'cause*
> *that's where the car seats are.* (p. 195)

Yet even at thirty-three months, Emily's grip on 'cause' words is still shaky. She has a vague notion of how to use *because* to represent a reason, but she still has difficulty linking the phrases in some kind of temporal order, and clarifying what caused what. (A baby brother was born prior to this monologue, one supposes around Christmastime. This is the "baby" she refers to.)

> "*We bought a baby, 'cause, the well, because, when*
> *she, well, we thought it was for Christmas*" [Meaning,
> "The reason we have this baby is because we bought it
> for a Christmas present." Notice how complex this is:
> *the reason is because*] She continues:

> "*but when we went to the store we didn't have our*
> *jacket on, but I saw some dolly, and I yelled at my*
> *mother and said I want one of those dolly. So after we*
> *were finished with the store, we went over to the dolly*
> *and she bought me one. So I have one.*" (p. 163)

Nelson uses this example to illustrate children's narratives and to point out Emily's advanced use of grammar. But it's also a clear example of the gradual shift from "use before meaning" to "meaning from use," and shows how long it takes for this to occur. *Because* sounds convincing in this sentence due to her fluency and her correct use of past tense verbs and time words (*when, after, finished*), which is very deceiving.

Nelson concludes from Emily's remarks that she is unconcerned about her new baby brother, and prefers to focus on everyday, mundane things. But I think what Emily says reveals intense concern. It goes without saying that young children find being displaced by a baby profoundly disturbing. Notice that in this monologue, "a baby" is the closest she gets to talking about him, and the *only* time she talks about him directly. As the monologue continues, Emily draws a fascinating analogy between the sudden appearance of a baby (something she can't understand) and a dolly (something she does understand). You buy dollies at stores, and you go into stores to buy presents at Christmas. Thus, the logic: Baby brother = dolly. Both can be bought at stores at Christmas. This explains where the baby must have come from.

Although this interpretation may not be the correct one, it's certainly worth exploring for Emily's parents. They could get into quite a dialogue over this issue, by asking questions like these:

> Your baby brother is a little like a dolly, isn't he?
> Do you think Ben really *is* a dolly?
> He does do some things that dollies don't do though. Can you think of some of those things?
> He cries all by himself, and he wiggles his arms by himself, just like you do.
> Dollies don't wiggle by themselves, do they?
> And he is going to grow big, just like you are growing big. Dollies don't grow big, do they?

Emily's parents could take this as far as they want to, connecting *baby brother* to Emily by having her think about what's alike between them, and disconnecting *baby brother* from *dolly* by looking at what's different. Of course, this could lead to questions that are fraught with difficulty, so parents need to be prepared: If baby brothers aren't bought in stores, then where do they come from? What does it mean to be alive?

Categorizing

We see that very early in her third year, Emily has the ability to talk to herself about possible analogies between things that look alike. As we know that babies are able to *think* in words long before they can say them, this means they must start making analogies much earlier. Humans are particularly talented at sorting out the world by putting things into groups that look alike or behave alike. This activity is called categorizing.

Emily's parents have a difficult problem: trying to get Emily to understand the difference between babies and dolls and the similarities between a baby and a two-year-old. Emily, at two, was already trying to make these comparisons in speech. Younger children will be making comparisons *before* they can talk about it. How can we get toddlers to show us what they notice about differences and similarities?

Visual Categorizing

PSYCHOLOGISTS HAVE answered this question with a simple game that you might want to try. Choose small objects from two categories with about four objects in each category. It doesn't matter what you use, but the four objects in each group need to be similar, same shape, same name, same function, same color, same size, and so forth, and the two categories should be very different. Here are some of the objects that have been used:

> four toy horses and four little pencils
> four flat yellow rectangles and four red human figures

four little boxes and four balls of clay
four small dolls and four red plastic cars

Mix them all up and put them on a table and watch what happens. At nine to ten months, the child picks up one toy at a time and plays with each one at random. Sometime between twelve and sixteen months, the child will handle or touch the objects that belong together, first one category and then the other. A few toddlers this age will spontaneously sort them into two piles. By eighteen months, nearly all children sort them into two piles. If your toddler is around fifteen to sixteen months, say, *Give them to me* or *Pick them all up* and hold out both your hands. The fifteen- to sixteen-month-old toddler would tend to give you one set, leaving the other set on the table. At around eighteen months, and certainly by the time of the vocabulary explosion, the child will efficiently collect up the objects in one category and put them in one hand, and put the remaining objects in your other hand. You can expand this game by adding one more category, especially if your child is a whiz at the two-category problem.

Categorization and Language

CATEGORIZING, GROUPING things by similarities and differences, is one of the main ways that children learn new words. They understand that a word they've never heard before probably stands for something that is unfamiliar. Here's another experiment to do with a child somewhere between the 50- and 100-word vocabulary level. It won't work before.

Put a pile of three or four categories of familiar toys on the table. Add some objects from an unfamiliar category and mix them together. For the unfamiliar category, small kitchen utensils is a good choice (can opener, small sieve, garlic press, and so forth, but nothing sharp). After your child has played with the toys for a while, say you're going to make them nice and tidy, and put them back neatly into categories: cars together, dollies together, blocks, fuzzy toys, puzzle pieces, and so forth. Put out the kitchen utensils as a group too. Now choose *one* from each group and put them in a row in front of the child, and ask: *"Can I have the car? . . . Can I have the dolly? . . . Can I have the lep?"* At this point, your child will hesitate, look up at you, examine the toys, and then reach for the utensil. Not having a word for those strange objects, she will work out that the strange new word must go with the strange objects. Keep playing the game until you have used up all the options.

In case you're worried that your child will go through life calling can openers and strainers *leps*, wait awhile and give her the right names for each object. Do this a few times, and she'll be fine. Toddlers and children up to around the age of five or six work on the principle: *What do I know? I'm just a dumb kid. I probably got that mixed up.*

These studies are convincing proof that one of the big myths about children's language development is false. This is the myth that the reason why children call all animals *doggie* and all men *daddy* is because they can't tell the difference between a dog and a cow, and between daddy and all other men. (I was taught this myth in college.) If a child can tell objects apart and sort them into two categories at sixteen months of age, they are not going to have any trouble telling a dog and a cow apart. But what are they really doing when they call other men *daddy*?

Imagine that you are still on Crypton, and after four months of patient listening and observing, you finally work out that when Cryptonians point to a particular tree, the one that grows the green stuff they use for food, they always say *schpplyg*. One day you are out for a walk with your guardian, and you see an amazing tree, one you have not seen before. It is covered with giant red balls, like Christmas tree ornaments. You try to get your guardian's attention, but it is distracted by something else. You blurt out the closest word you know, *schpplyg*, and point to the tree. It's the best you can do. It works. And you learn something too. This isn't a *schpplyg*, it's a *ddrspwubt*, the latter word spoken with a shrill, rising intonation.

A toddler does exactly the same thing. Think about how different the myth is (that toddlers are too underdeveloped to tell dogs and cows apart) from what your child is actually doing. First he registers something new he has never seen before. He knows he doesn't have a word for it, even in his thoughts. He rummages through his mind for something that's the closest match to what he sees, something that *looks most like* what he doesn't have a word for. It's the same type of backward reasoning you use when you're writing a letter and forget how to spell a word. If you're too lazy to get the dictionary, you search through your mind for a synonym that you *can* spell.

The toddler's train of thought goes something like this:

> *"Well, that's something quite new. Hmm. What could it be? It flies up in the sky. It's very small. It is yellow all over. I only know one name for something that flies in the sky, but I've never seen a yellow one. That's the only word I know, so I'll say that word."*

At this point, your super bright toddler gets your attention, points to a butterfly, and says, *little birdie*. This is your opportunity to teach a new word and a new concept: "No, that's a butterfly. Butterflies are too small to be birdies. They don't have feathers like birdies."

Hierarchical Categories

ADULTS USE hierarchical category systems to classify things: plant, tree, deciduous tree, beech, copper beech. Children don't understand classification systems until they're around five years old. *Tree* in this sequence is known as a 'basic level' category word. And although mom is not aware of it, most of what she teaches are basic level words. Typical basic level words are *dog, tree, flower, car, chair*. Moms seldom use subordinate category words with young children: *cocker spaniel, oak, rhododendron, Buick*, and *rocking chair*. Nor do they use superordinate category words: *animals, plants, vehicles,* or *furniture*.

Basic level words contain the most information, and they're also the most useful, not too specific and not too global or vague. This means your toddler can easily use one of these words for a similar object. If you tell your toddler that *that* dog is a Labrador, she's not going to get much practice with this word. How many Labradors will she see in a week or month? And it creates another problem, because she would have to learn a different name for every dog she saw. Pretty overwhelming. On the other hand, if you point to a dog and say *animal*, then what will you call a cow, a cat, a pig, or a horse?

Despite the fact that parents stick to basic level words most of the time, they don't do this with highly familiar objects and routines. They use basic level, subordinate, and superordinate category words all the time, and, surprisingly, so do children. Mothers ask, "Do you want a drink?" *Drink* is a superordinate category word meaning "anything edible, liquid, and goes in a glass or a cup." If she gets a nod or a *yes*, then mom asks for a basic level word: "What do you want to drink?" The child knows immediately that the request is for a basic level word for that category. He never answers *horse* or *banana*.

If he answers *doose* (instead of milk or water), mom has the option to move to the subordinate level and get more specific: "You can have apple juice or orange juice. Do you want apple juice?" If he signals *no*, then she asks: "Do you want orange juice?" *Toys* is another example of a superordinate category word. It has several subdivisions as well: toys in the toy box, bath toys, and cuddly toys. Each toy category has many basic level words: cars, puzzles, blocks, balls / ducks, boats / Teddy, kitty, Pooh.

Children show us that they know a lot about hierarchical categories by the way they behave, but they have a hard time sorting this out verbally without some help from mom. Here is an example of twenty-two-month-old Emily's unsuccessful attempt to solve this puzzle:

I like food, and muffins too!

The Threshold of the Story World

By the end of the second year of life, your toddler has become a mental whiz. She is able to understand much of what you say to her, sort out the differences and similarities between objects in the world, ponder the meaning of the not-now past and the not-now future, wonder why things happen the way they do, and say around 300 to 400 words.

When you think about it, the toddler spends much of the second year of life developing the skills she needs to enter 'the story world.' Early on, she creates her own theater in pretend play, demonstrating her vague understanding of real and unreal. She pushes hard at breaking boundaries, knowing that fantasy is fun and can even be funny. She begins to understand self and other. Her budding sense of empathy makes her aware of other people's needs and desires, and that they can be different from her own. Without empathy, a child can't relate to a character in a story unless she believes that the character is really her in disguise. She knows about a not-now future world in which things might happen, or will happen, but haven't happened yet. She knows about a not-now past in which things happened that affected the now, and is beginning to use past tense by the end of the second year. She understands (but doesn't know she understands) time past and time present, because her memory capacity is expanding rapidly. (Recall that eighteen-month-olds can remember a single strange event for at least four months.) At the same time, she is struggling to come to grips with causes and reasons for why things happen the way they do. She thinks categorically about what is alike and what is different, and begins to make analogies, even though she may not talk about them until she's almost three.

Now think about the story world. It is a world of the imagination where the real can be stretched to the limit until it becomes the unreal. Teddies, dollies, and action men can talk, move around by themselves, fix dinner, and go on adventures. All stories have a story line, which simply means a *time line*. Every story, from the most simple to the most complex, is about structuring time. In *Jack and the Beanstalk*, Jack grows beans, *then* one beanstalk grows very big, *then* he climbs it, *then* he comes to a castle, *then* he figures out a way to get in, *then* he sees the giant, and so forth. Children love *Jack and the Beanstalk*, not because of the underlying themes of overcoming poverty, hunger, and oppression, but because it marches through time in such an imaginative way.

Stories are riddled with reasons and causes: *Why* did Hansel and Gretel get taken into the forest? *Why* didn't it work to drop breadcrumbs to mark their path? Did this *reason cause* them to get lost? *Why* did the wicked witch turn all the children into gingerbread? Once again, the underlying themes of poverty, hunger, abandonment, and death have no meaning for the child. Instead, it is the *why* of everything that happens in the story that captures their attention, and not knowing what will happen next.

Children's stories manipulate category boundaries so the familiar becomes unfamiliar. The big, bad wolf is still a wolf even though he is in grandma's bed, wearing her nightgown and cap. The reader knows this, but for some reason Little Red Riding Hood does not.

Stories are written in past tense: Once upon a time—. The present tense is hardly ever used, and when it is, it merely describes the pictures that march a child through a routine: *Teddy gets into bed. Teddy goes to sleep. Teddy gets up. Teddy brushes his teeth.* Annotated pictures aren't stories, though it's fun for very young children to follow a familiar routine when the main character (which is really them) looks like an animal or a fuzzy toy.

Children love to be read to, even before they understand most of the words. For very young children, this is because they like the sound of your voice and the cadences and rhythms of storytelling. Children from around age two and up will listen in rapt attention to a story they've heard many times, and then ask for it to be repeated again and *again* and **again.** Parents are baffled by this, because it's such a bore to them. Parents imagine that, with all this repetition, their child must be memorizing the story verbatim, and certainly getting the story sequence down pat. But it turns out that the reason children like hearing a story over and over is precisely *because they can't remember it.* A young child's story memory is in the twilight zone between total amnesia and vague recollection. The repetition is actually quite stimulating, because the story sounds vaguely familiar each time they hear it, yet they continue to be surprised by what happens next. Nothing captures our interest more than something familiar yet surprising or not quite known. This is why music lovers can listen to the same symphony or the same opera over and over again.

The message for now, I'm afraid, is repeat, repeat, repeat, if that is what your child desires. You also have to bear in mind that many of the words will be unfamiliar, and we know for sure that repetition is the key to vocabulary building. When the child is older, you can enhance story memory with a few tricks, but not at this age.

A Parent's Guide

Mind Your Communication Style

IF YOU HAVEN'T done so before, read the final section in Chapter 1. This provides some excellent advice on the most productive ways to communicate with your child, and these guidelines don't change much over the years. For a child in her second year of life, here are some other suggestions.

THE SPORTSCASTER MODE

Are you a sportscaster? Do you provide running commentary when your child is at play and you're watching? Monitor yourself for a week when you're sitting with your child as he plays, and listen to what you say. If you're not a sportscaster, that's okay. There's no particular reason to change what you're doing. For those parents who are, sportscasting seems to be an excellent way to build vocabulary, though there's no concrete proof of this. You are providing the exact words to describe your child's actions *as he's performing them.* And there's the added bonus of talking about something he is obviously interested in, so you have his attention. Of course, parents should never get stuck in this mode. There must be mutual play and communicative interactions as well.

Use Infant-Directed Talk

Children learn language when talk is directed *to them* and not to somebody else, what psychologists call "infant-directed talk." Monitor yourself for two or three days and note what you do. How much time do you spend on the phone? How much time do you spend talking to a neighbor or friend, even one who brings her child to play with yours? How much time do you talk to dad or the other kids? This is a matter of proportion; baby should never get all the attention. Just remember that a child is learning essentially nothing when adults talk to each other or to older children. Have you ever wondered why your child gets so frustrated when you talk too long on the phone or to a friend over coffee? His annoying clinging, tugging on your clothes, and loud whining isn't so much because he's demanding and must have you all to himself; it's because he can't understand anything you're saying. For a toddler, it's like spending hours in gobbledegook land.

Clarify Causality

Toward the end of the second year, 'why' questions start appearing, or, occasionally, even 'deep questions,' like *Where do you get babies?* You are being asked to supply causes and reasons. Watch yourself. If Emma sees dad dressed up in an all-white tennis ensemble, and asks: *Why Daddy got new clothes?* Don't say something like this: *Daddy's wearing those clothes because Uncle John asked him to play tennis.* First, and most importantly, the word *because* doesn't mean anything to a child this young. (Nor does *tennis* in this hypothetical case.) Second, phrasing the sentence this way doesn't make a clear causal link between clothes and tennis. Third, in *because* sentences, causality is backwards in time (effect precedes cause), making this link even harder to grasp.

Try something like this instead: *Well, Uncle John asked Daddy to play tennis. Tennis is a game you play with a ball. People usually wear white clothes to play tennis.* What you're doing here is turning time around and putting it in the right sequence, while providing some helpful cues about words and concepts. You could add something like: *Would you like to go see Daddy and Uncle John play tennis?* This way the child can see what you're talking about.

TEACH NEW NAMES FOR UNFAMILIAR THINGS

You're out for a walk in the woods on a Sunday morning and spot some cows in a field. Mr. Observant in the stroller shouts:

Big doggies. *Look, Mommy,* **big doggies!**

Think before you speak. Is there any way you can link the cows to something in your child's experience? You notice that the cows are the same color as your brown Lab, Bartholomew. Give Mr. Observant credit for this.

> Oh yes, look over there. There are lots of *cows* (loud and prolonged). They are brown like Bartholomew. But they're *cows*, not dogs. *Cows* are much bigger than dogs. Can you say *cow*?

ENTERING THE STORY WORLD

There are two important things to remember about reading stories. (1) the experience should be enjoyable for your child, and (2) the child needs help with her story memory. To insure enjoyment, don't interrupt stories as you read them. Don't try to explain everything and define words as you go. Children love the flow of it—the modulated storyteller voice, even if they don't understand most of the words. If you're asked to read a favorite story over and over, take advantage of this. Read the story through in the normal way. Then go back and pick out a character or place or event that's important to the story. Turn back to the page where the important character first appears and look at the picture. Talk about what this character looks like, what he's wearing. If it's an animal, tell your child what it is. Talk about where the character is—what place is it? Where did he come from? Why did he go to this place? Where is he going next? After spending a few minutes on this, read the story again (if it's short) in the usual way. Next time, focus on something else, an event, like why all the puppies fell out of the boat. What made that happen?

What Does Your Child Know?

IN ADDITION TO your daily word chart, there are all sorts of other things your child can do that you might want to check out.

POINTING

At this age your child should be pointing to share what she sees with you. A point gesture involves another person's cooperation. The child has to get mom's attention, look directly at the interesting object while pointing to it and talking about it, and check to see if you're looking too. This is a very complex act, as you can see. The obvious way to check this out is to note if your child spontaneously points to something. But you could also try this little game. We'll call it: Mommy Sees, Baby Sees.

Start out by saying, "Look, Mommy sees a ball." Then point and ask, "Do you see the ball? Do you see the ball, Sally?" Now it's Sally's turn, so you say, "What can Sally see? What can you see, Sally?" If Sally joins the game, watch what she does. Does she point to an object like you did? Does she watch your face to see if you're looking at it? If Sally is a little slow catching on, you can take a few more turns. If she doesn't get it, wait until she's a little older.

DOES YOUR CHILD USE FROZEN PHRASES?

What type of speaker is your child? Pick a time when your child is most alert and most talkative. Write down all the words your child says within a fixed time period (thirty to sixty minutes). Do this for several days. Then count all the common nouns (not pronouns), and all the frozen phrases, like *all-gone, there-it-is, oh-oh-down*, and total them up. Divide the number of frozen phrases by this total, and this will give you the proportion or percent of frozen phrases. Remember, for the majority of children, this proportion is around 25 percent or less. If your child scores 50 percent or higher, he or she is a frozen phrase child, a child who builds language as much or more by phrases as by individual words. Monitor this over time (if it interests you) to see if this proportion holds up. Remember, we still don't know whether one style builds language faster than the other over the long term—and even if we did, there's nothing you can do about it.

DOES YOUR CHILD USE FUNCTION WORDS?

Here's a simpler version of the 'gub dog' experiment reported earlier. Don't try this experiment until your child is around sixteen to eighteen months. Cut out four pictures from magazines. One of them should be of a dog. Put them in a row in front of your child and ask: "Can you find *was* dog for Mommy?" Watch what happens. Now scramble the order of the pictures and ask: "Can you find *the* dog for Mommy?" Your child should have much more trouble with the first request than the second, showing that she is very familiar with *the* and what it implies.

To check out your child's ability to categorize objects or to empathize with your tastes in food, you can repeat the 'broccoli' and the 'leps' studies discussed earlier.

3.

The Outrageous, Self-Propelling, Parent-Defying, Simply Amazing, Terrific Twos

FOR TWO YEARS YOU HAVE DONE EVERYTHING RIGHT. YOU are well on your way to raising the perfect child. Then your loving, cuddly, budding genius, with his 100 percent intelligible vocabulary of 385 words, the paragon who puts his toys in the toy box on request, who eats entire meals without dropping bits on the floor, that sensible, cautious little pal, who sticks to you like Clingwrap in shopping malls, the supermarket, and the hardware store, suddenly looses his cling and begins to live by his rules, not yours.

Two-year-olds march to their own drummer. They are notable for their intense, focused look, which they wear most of the day, as if what they're about to do is the most important thing in the world. And what they want to do often excludes mom and dad, brothers, sisters, baby-sitters, and other interfering persons, anyone who impedes their freedom to pursue important goals.

You realize something is amiss the day Jimmy makes mud pies out of dog chow, pieces of bittersweet cooking chocolate,

and *real* mud, and feeds them to Robespierre the dog. You ponder on this uncharacteristic behavior as you sit at the vet's office.
Jimmy had explained his reasoning very precisely.

WHAT ARE YOU DOING?
Feed Robey.
WHY ARE YOU FEEDING HIM MUD?
DOGS DON'T EAT MUD!
Robey hungry. My feed Robey.
[At that point Robey whined in pain.]
NOW LOOK! YOU MADE ROBEY SICK.
WE HAVE TO TAKE HIM TO THE VET.
[Blank stare.]
DON'T YOU EVER DO THIS AGAIN.
DO YOU HEAR ME?
[Blank stare.]

He probably won't do this again; he'll do something else instead.
While some two-year-olds stay sunny and sociable, others can
become solemn, secretive, and unpredictable, and parents need
to know why. This is the first time in the child's life when he is
truly in control of his body, his mind, and his environment, and
can act on his plans and desires. Sometimes, the change is quite
overwhelming, and in case you're feeling down and out for the
count, this 'two' shall pass.

To make you feel better, I've prepared a 'top this' list of
imprudent scientific experiments mainly from my personal experience to let you know you're not alone. And for those smug
readers who escape this fate and think it's due to their superior
parenting skills, just have another child and you might not be so
lucky. I should add that while I don't have the statistics on this
one, the 'top this' list contains many more boy escapades than

girl escapades—reasons unknown. Boys tend to be oriented to the world of objects, exploring the world firsthand, in physical action; boys behave more like physicists. Girls are oriented to social interactions and more likely to learn through questions and asking for reasons; girls behave more like psychologists. These trends or tendencies will have an impact on a child's mental representation of the world and on vocabulary development.

'Top This' List of Imprudent Scientific Experiments

Chemistry

The Nature of Liquids and Substances That Dissolve or Transmute

Experiment 1. Drop several lengths of toilet paper, or the entire toilet roll, plus other objects (washcloth, toothpaste tube) into the toilet bowl. Flush. Results: Objects that dissolve in liquid will go down the drain; objects that don't will clog the toilet.

Experiment 2. Apparatus: Bucket, large stick or spoon. Put several ingredients into bucket, such as scouring powder, coffee grounds, leftover breakfast cereal, polyfill for caulking cracks in walls, etc. Add something liquid (cold coffee, water, milk, etc.). Stir vigorously. Results: Polyfill binds this mixture very nicely. The bucket cannot be reused. When asked about these experiments, the scientist replied, *I mix it up.* When questioned further, he replied, *I put it in.*

The Nature of Color Masking and Absorption

Experiment 3. This was carried out on Christmas Day, just after Christmas dinner, about 4:00 p.m. Adults seated at the table absorbed in conversation. (It isn't necessary to do this experiment on Christmas Day, but it is essential that everyone but the scientist is fully engaged in something else.) Apparatus: Sister's new set of finger paints (Christmas present), available furniture. Unscrew the lid of a jar with a color that contrasts nicely to color of upholstery on the furniture. Apply paint with fingers and palms to upholstery in broad strokes. Results: Bright red finger paint masks sage green of upholstery completely. It will not wash off. It cannot be removed in any way. [There were no further experiments on color, as this two-year-old was lucky to escape with his life.]

Physics

MECHANICS

Experiment 1. Purpose: To explore the nature and construction of mechanical devices like clocks. Apparatus: All clocks in the house. Procedure: Work in silence, out of sight, and undetected. Proceed one clock at a time. Remove outer screws first, and then small inner screws. Slowly dismantle clock. Lay out component parts systematically, because they will be reassembled. Reassemble clock. Watch clock to see if hands move. They do not. [This ongoing experiment went undetected until every clock in the house had failed. The watchmaker who subsequently repaired the clocks reported that each clock had been taken apart and put back together almost, *but not quite*, correctly.]

GRAVITY AND DURABILITY OF OBJECTS IN FREE FALL

Experiment 2. Purpose: To explore the consequences of the force of gravity on an object tilted at an angle and released into free fall. [Note: This was not a replication of a study measuring the comparable speed of *two* objects in free fall, like Galileo's experiment at the leaning tower of Pisa.] This experiment is carried out on any object that can be tilted by a two-year-old. Best choices are coffee tables, wooden chairs. Results: Coffee-table legs break, chair legs loosen but do not break. [This scientist was caught in the act when one of these experiments was ongoing. He explained his purpose succinctly: *I wanna see if it break.*]

Exploration

THE NATURE OF DISAPPEARANCE

Experiment 1. How to disappear in a department store. Wait until no one is looking. Climb inside a rack of clothes. Round racks are preferable. Stand there silently. When you are called, do not move or cry out. Keep this up for as long as possible. Results: The explorer/disappearer was spotted by small pair of shoes attached to chubby legs visible below the hemlines of the clothes on the rack. Now the game is up and won't have the same impact again.

Experiment 2. How to escape in order to explore desirable locations not visible from the home or yard. Wait until no one is looking. Open door or gate latch, or squeeze through fence. Run as fast as possible in the intended direction. Results: This experiment was a failure. A neighbor spotted the small, racing figure and hopped into his car seconds after hearing mom's screams. The escapee explorer was headed off at the next crossroad. When questioned about his actions and where he intended to go, the explorer was in no doubt: *I go see dee cars.*

It's Not Just About Science. What's Really Going On?

THE SECRET scientific experiments were secret, because the children knew they would be stopped. But two-year-olds are equally well known for their bravura and overt defiance. They can be uncompromisingly negative when it suits them:

> Come on, we have to get your brother from school.
> *NO!*
> You can't stay here alone. You have to come with me, so put on your coat.
> *WON'T!*

They are notable for their candor:

> Say hello to Mrs. Cadbury.
> *NO.*
> Why won't you say hello to Mrs. Cadbury?
> She likes little girls.
> *I don't like Miz Cadby. She has big teeth.*

They overtly court displeasure. Researchers recorded these examples from their own children's behavior, acts carried out in the full glare of mom or dad's withering gaze.

"Our two-year-old didn't even look at the lamp cord (a forbidden object). Instead, his hand went out to touch it as he looked, steadily, gravely, and with great deliberation, at me."

"One of our children would move closer and closer to the forbidden object in geometrically precise increments, until she was only millimeters away from it, staring at her father all the time."

The scientists had a theory about this. During the first two years of life, children learn that people have different and conflicting desires, but that *parents always win*. Tugging on lamp cords is a no-no, and children must obey. If the child doesn't want a particularly noxious mashed-vegetable concoction, he has to eat it anyway. Two-year-olds are testing their muscle in these do-don't conflicts. So they taunt you. They try to do forbidden things *because you don't want them to*, as a test of your resolve. They stare at you because *your reaction* is more important than the forbidden act. There's another reason as well, which has to do with testing boundaries and parents' consistency in responding: *How much can I get away with here? I didn't get away with this last time, but what happens if I try again?*

I have stressed behavioral issues, because 'behavior' is what two-year-olds are all about. Keeping track of a two-year-old is not a party. Two-year-olds need their space, but they need your 'talk' as well. Join in at playtime, keep the chat going at meals and bedtime. This is the year that children reach the last rung on the language ladder and learn to speak in grammatically correct sentences.

Language at Two

Keeping Score

I AM PROVIDING some language milestones for two-year-olds. These are averages for children aged twenty-four to thirty-six months. The variability between children is just as great in the third year as it has been so far, so don't worry too much if your child doesn't measure up. I'll address the problem of late talkers in the next section.

If you're keeping a diary, or you're a keen 'language watcher,' you might want to check these statistics against your child. The average spoken vocabulary is 300 words at twenty-four months, 550 words at thirty months, and over 1,000 words at thirty-six months. Consonants are more difficult to produce than vowels and come in later. Clear pronunciation of some consonant contrasts like /w/ and /r/ (*wing, ring*), /s/ and /sh/ (*Sue, shoe*), may not appear until age five or six. (Individual sounds, called 'phonemes,' are indicated within slash marks.)

The average consonant repertoire at twenty-four months is eleven initial consonants: /b/, /p/, /t/, /d/, /g/, /k/, /m/, /n/, /h/, /w/, /s/ and five final consonants: /p/, /t/, /k/, /n/, /s/. These are the tallies for one-at-a-time consonants. It is rare to hear two-year-olds pronouncing adjacent consonants correctly in words like *black, trip, spoon, tank, help, friend*. One consonant is usually dropped or fudged: *bwack, tip, poon, tak, hep, fend*. The last consonants to appear are /f/, /v/, /z/, /sh/, /ch/, /j/, /th/, /ng/, /l/, /r/. Once again, these are averages, and the range at twenty-four months is huge, from three to sixteen initial consonants, and zero to eleven final consonants.

Children twenty-four months old were taped during a play session with their mothers, and the number of syllable types was tallied for each child. The percent of children who produced these consonant and vowel syllable patterns was as follows (with examples in parentheses):

CV, V, CVC (*do, Oh, dog*)	97%
CVCV (*ba-by*)	79%
CVCVC (*do-nut*)	65%
CCV (*cry*)	58%
CVCC (*won't*)	48%

This tally doesn't reflect how often these patterns appeared in conversations, merely that they appeared. There is a strong connection between the number of consonants produced correctly and the size of a child's spoken vocabulary. This means that the aptitude for producing individual speech sounds controls the number of words the child can say, and hence productive vocabulary size. One reason for a small spoken vocabulary could be due to a delay in speech-motor development. But keep in mind that a child's spoken vocabulary may bear little relationship to her *receptive* vocabulary (the words she understands).

Late Talkers

SOME PARENTS WORRY unduly if their child lags behind in language development. But nothing is more unpredictable than children's spoken language. Parents should take comfort in the fact that nearly everyone learns to speak just fine. Even severely mentally retarded people can carry on a conversation. The human brain is geared to produce an efficient talking machine, no matter how long it takes.

A survey on 38,000 children, ages six to eighteen years, individually tested for speech accuracy, showed that the number of children with fully accurate speech continued to increase to the highest age tested. At age six, the proportion of children with speech problems rated 'severe' was 12 percent for boys and 7 percent for girls. But this dropped sharply by age eight (3 percent for both sexes), and by age twelve, it was a mere 1 percent. The most consistent finding is that speech-motor problems, on their own, are rarely cause for concern. They either self-correct or respond well to speech therapy. And there seems to be no time limits on improving speech clarity.

Recently, there has been a spate of studies on late talkers, those children who lag well behind their peers in spoken language. One of the most fascinating studies happened by accident. A team of researchers was investigating language development in 13-month-old children. The children were normal in their onset of babbling, the size of their receptive vocabulary, and their hearing. They were tested on receptive and expressive vocabulary every three months until they were twenty-five months old.

By the second or third visit, it was obvious that four of the thirty-two children in the study were falling so far behind that they were a cause for concern. Although there had been no intention to investigate late talkers, this was a unique opportunity, and these children were tracked for an additional year. The contrast between the late talkers and the other children was very noticeable by nineteen months. The average vocabulary size was 135 words. For late talkers, it was 16 words. The gap got wider with time: 264 words versus 29 at twenty-two months, and 442 words versus 54 at twenty-five months. It seemed obvious to everyone that the late talkers were headed for trouble. Imagine their surprise when they saw what happened over the next year. The size of spoken vocabulary for each late talker is shown below.

At thirty-four months, the late talkers' spoken vocabulary was in the normal range, and receptive vocabulary was actually above normal. They could find no reason for the delay. Speech

SPOKEN VOCABULARY FOR FOUR LATE TALKERS
Age in Months

	13	16	19	22	25	28	31	34
CHILD A	6	5	17	41	51	273	579	646
CHILD B	5	16	34	43	87	107	122	369
CHILD C	0	1	8	15	52	216	563	623
CHILD D	3	4	6	18	25	214	542	542

accuracy was not the problem. The repertoire of consonants and vowels was normal at age two, and speech intelligibility was high. Clearly, these children were not held back by problems with articulation. The scientists concluded that patterns of early language development do not predict later development. But questions remain. How common are late talkers? At what age does a language delay predict problems later on?

When various researchers looked at the incidence of late talkers in the population, the numbers were much higher than expected. In one study, all the children between twenty-two and twenty-six months in an entire town were tested. A cut-off of *fewer than 50 spoken words* was used to define a late talker. They found this applied to 14 percent of the children. When they added a second marker: *fewer than 50 words **and** no word combinations*, the incidence was largely unchanged. They also found a sex difference, which has been confirmed in every study on late talkers. Late talkers are mainly boys—over 70 percent in all studies. There is a sex difference in vocabulary size as well, with girls having larger vocabularies.

When the results are combined from a number of studies, the incidence of late talkers (fewer than 50 words at age two) ranges between 10 percent and 14 percent. Because boys predominate, this represents *14 percent to 20 percent of all boys,* but only *6 percent to 8 percent of all girls.* These rates are much too high to be abnormal, a point emphasized by every scientist in the field. They believe that late talkers are just 'late bloomers.' Nevertheless, when late talkers are followed to age three, about 50 percent 'bloom' and 50 percent do not. No language measure, like percent consonants spoken correctly, number of two-word utterances per hour, the mean number of words per utterance, and so on, seems to predict who will bloom and who won't.

Unfortunately, late talkers have not been followed past the

age of three. Instead, at around age four, speech and language delays become the province of clinical specialists in the speech and hearing sciences, and their focus is on diagnosis and remediation. Yet, even scientists in the research arm of this discipline also report that language development is unpredictable. We know that speech clarity continues to improve over a long period of time, but vocabulary size and grammar can also shoot into the normal range after the age of five. So far, no one knows how to predict which children will have long-term language problems.

A Plan of Action

NEEDLESS TO SAY, given the fact that experts can't predict language development until age five or older, I don't have the perfect plan of action for what you should do if your child is lagging far behind. It's a good idea to get your child's hearing tested in the first year of life, especially if you have concerns. If your child is prone to earaches, get hearing tests frequently. Some language delays are caused by poor hearing, which makes people's speech sound fuzzy and indistinct, and difficult for the child to reproduce.

If your child doesn't understand much of what you say, ask your pediatrician for advice, or see a licensed speech and language therapist. The most serious marker is a very low *receptive* vocabulary score. Children who don't understand what people say have the worst prognosis. If your child is *seriously* delayed in spoken language at age three compared to the norms described above, arrange for a complete battery of language tests from a licensed speech and language therapist. Testing must include measures of receptive language to be meaningful.

Follow the experts' advice, but guard against having your child labeled. I recommend that you don't share information about a diagnosis with your child's preschool or school. If you schedule sessions with a speech and language therapist, think of your child as needing extra help, in the same way he might need extra help with handwriting and forming letters correctly. When parents and teachers believe a child has a language impairment, this can have a profound impact on the child's academic progress. There are many reasons for this. Parents and teachers tend to expect less and make excuses for the child. Many schools put these children in special classes. With few exceptions, special education is notorious for having perfected the art of 'dumbed-down learning,' the exact opposite of what a child with a language delay needs. As a result, children get further behind in their schoolwork, which puts them at extra risk for emotional and psychological difficulties.

Nancy Cohen investigated the incidence of language impairments in children referred to two mental health clinics in Toronto for behavioral and emotional problems. She tested all the children referred over a two-year period on a battery of language tests, and found that 64 percent met the criteria for a language impairment. This is a very high proportion indeed, and shows that poor communication skills contribute to social, emotional, and behavioral problems. But her most important finding was the power of a label. Half the children with poor language skills had been diagnosed with a language impairment previously and everyone knew they had a problem. The other half had never been tested and no one thought there was anything wrong with them. These children were reading normally, doing well academically, and had high academic self-esteem. The children who had been diagnosed as language impaired were reading at least two years below grade level and were in serious trouble academically. When Cohen compared the language test scores of these two groups of children, *they did not differ statistically on any test.* In other words, it wasn't the severity of the language problem that caused the poor reading skills. And although one can't say for certain that the diagnosis *caused* the reading problem, it is hard to imagine what else might have caused it. Children identified as language impaired are more likely to end up in remedial or special classes where teachers expect too little from them, and they don't get the right kind of instruction.

This is cutting edge research, and we have a long way to go before we get these issues sorted out. Parents should be cautious about prejudging the situation, adopting a diagnosis too early, or sharing that diagnosis with the school.

The Grammar Magician

By twenty-four months, children are growing out of the two-word phase, and are well into the telegraphic speech mode. 'Telegraphic speech' is speech reduced to essential words, but it isn't like a real telegram. While the word order is correct, the grammar is not. Verbs are in present tense. Verb endings are missing, as are pronouns, plurals, and possessives, which makes the child's statements highly ambiguous and decidedly context dependent.

My go picnic. Big park.

Meaning, "I went to a picnic in a big park last Saturday" OR "I want to go on a picnic in the big park."

Mommy take it box.

Meaning, "Mommy took my toy box and put it away" OR "Mommy got a box from a store" OR "Mommy, get my toy box

out of the closet" OR "Mommy took away the box I was playing with."

As always, parents work hard at interpretation, but here's
some advice: Correcting grammar is NOT the way to exercise a
child's grammar muscle. If you try to have this kind of conversation, it will get you nowhere.

> *Mommy take it box.*
> No, dear. Say, Mommy took my box. Listen: Mommy—
> **TOOK—MY**—box. Now you say it.
> *Mommy take it box.*
> No—Mommy **TOOK**—say **TOOK.**
> *Took.*
> Good. Now say, Mommy took my box.
> *Mommy take it box.*

Research shows that parents almost never correct their children's
grammar (probably because they have too many conversations
like this one), and they only rephrase an incorrect sentence about
20 percent of the time. Despite the fact that parents seem to pay
little direct attention to grammar, nearly all children learn to
speak in grammatically correct sentences. Yet children can't do
this without parents' input. The important question is what kind
of input should this be?

First, parents need to speak in grammatically correct and
complete sentences. Your child will be learning the grammar
model that you provide. Second, if the child makes a grammatical error, rephrase what the child *meant* to say or should have
said. This gives her a direct model for a sentence she might have
used, *and* lets her know you understood her. Next, take the
opportunity to embellish and expand meaning, and engage her
in a conversation.

Mommy take it box.
Yes, Mommy took the box because I don't want you to break it. We got the box at the grocery store, didn't we? Do you know why we got this box?
Clothes.
Yes, we're going to take your baby clothes to the church. You're too big for these clothes now. You're not a baby anymore, are you? *[WAIT for response.]* The church will give the clothes to little babies who need them. Do you want to help the little babies get some clothes? Will you help me put the clothes in the box?

Notice what is happening here. Mom rephrases what the child's statement actually meant, then gives reasons for why she took the box away. She asks five questions to make sure the child understood what she did and why she did it. *Are you? Do you? Will you? Didn't we?* All elicit verification: *Are you understanding this?* She invites the child to participate in using the box for a good purpose, not just as a plaything. She doesn't order or demand it.

The most amazing thing about the third year of life is that children advance from saying things like *Mommy take it box* to complete sentences that come close to the complexity and accuracy of mom's reply. This is quite remarkable, especially when mom and dad don't correct grammar or speak in simple three- and four-word sentences. The mom in the example uses simple, common words, but she doesn't stint on past and future tense, verbs, contractions, pronouns, and prepositions.

What Is Grammar?

THE SHORT ANSWER to this question is that grammar is the structural organization of words in a clause or sentence of a particular language. Syntax refers to word order in a sentence, and morphology refers to things like prefixes and suffixes that mark verb tense, plurals, and so forth. Syntax + morphology = a grammar. English has a word order grammar with the structure of agent-action-object. Word order is quite arbitrary from one language to another. In German, the verb goes at the end: 'The policeman the robber arrested has.' A language learner has the job of figuring out what kinds of words go where in a sentence.

This short answer tells us nothing about how children learn a grammar or even what it is for. Noam Chomsky, a famous linguist, went furthest in trying to solve this problem. He recognized that children could never learn a grammar by memorizing every sentence they ever heard. Children can understand sentences they have never heard before, and can produce sentences that no one ever heard before. Nor could they do this by memorizing rules, for the simple reason that most parents don't know grammatical rules, and those who do would have a difficult time explaining them to a child. For these reasons, there has to be a common structure underlying all grammars, not a set of unique rules for each language like those that grammarians conjure up—which sounds like this:

'The present participle (ongoing action) requires the auxiliary verb *to be* as in *John is running down the street*. The auxiliary verb takes the same tense as the main verb (John *is*). To form a question, the auxiliary verb is moved to the head of the sentence, while the present participle remains in position following the subject, as in *Is John running down the street?*'

Chomsky's great insight was to reduce this complexity to a basic foundation that worked for all languages, what he called a "universal grammar." He coined the term "phrase structure grammar'" to describe this. There are two main types of phrases in every sentence in every grammar in every language: a noun phrase and a verb phrase.

There are numerous clues to help identify noun and verb phrases.

- In English, a noun is usually signaled by a marker, called an article: *a* or *the*. It can also be signaled by a descriptor, called an adjective. Adjectives follow articles and precede nouns ('the apple pie' and *not* 'the pie of apple,' as in French). Where the article or adjective sits in a sentence is a cue to a noun phrase.
- The first phrase in a sentence is usually a noun phrase and most commonly the subject of the sentence: *Boats* come adrift from their moorings in these storms.
- The first phrase + *an article* signal a noun and probably the subject of the sentence: *The boat* came adrift from its mooring.
- The first phrase + an article + *a descriptor* (adjective) signal a noun and probably the subject of the sentence: *The yellow boat* came adrift from its mooring.

In other words, there are three cues that cooperate to signal a noun phrase and the subject of the sentence.

Verb phrases follow the subject of the sentence, verb descriptors (adverbs) take the suffix *ly*, and adverbs usually *follow* verbs: The car spun *wildly*—but not always: 'The leaves swirled and *gently* floated onto the pond.' These patterns of order within order provide multiple ways to signal a noun phrase and a verb phrase.

Nevertheless, this doesn't solve the problem of *how* a child learns this structure. Obviously, two-year-olds don't know the words *noun* or *verb*, and no one could possibly explain this to a child. In any case, the English language conspires against them. Many English words are chameleons; they can be a noun, a verb, or an adjective: 'He *cut* off the branch and got a *cut* on his hand.' 'He decided to *open* the window, and he stared out the *open* window.' Despite this, children have no trouble learning which words go where in a sentence.

A child's mastery of grammar is based on three main abilities: vocabulary, categorizing, and verbal memory. The primary skill in understanding and producing grammatical sentences is vocabulary. A child may never know what a noun, verb, or adjective is, but she will certainly know *words* for persons, animals, places, things, and *words* for actions (whether past, present, or future), and *words* for appearances (colors, size, shape, etc.).

Infants begin to be aware of perceptual categories (animals, cars, food) around three to four months. By eighteen months, children begin to *spontaneously* categorize objects during play (all the marbles here, all the blocks there), as we saw in Chapter 2. Vocabulary builds in tandem with categorizing. As categorizing skill improves, the categories become more detailed, and more labels are needed: all the green marbles; all the big blocks; all the big, green marbles; and all the little, yellow ones. Words are categorized by *what* they refer to and describe. The 'thing' (noun) contains its attribute. 'Green' is a property of the marbles; marble is not a property of green. 'Big' is a property of the blocks. Verbs are what these persons, animals, objects *do*. Places don't 'do' anything, they are somewhere you are or somewhere you go. Understanding these distinctions is simply knowing *more* about reference, like kind, and difference.

To produce a sentence, the child has to order these different kinds of words. At one level she already knows the order, having heard an endless number of correctly produced sentences by the time she reaches the two-word stage.

The most important rule of conversations is not a grammar rule, but the rule that *you must communicate something*. And while mothers rarely correct grammar, they enforce this rule a lot. A two-year-old won't get by with the sentence: *The dog.* Mom is going to say: "What dog?" or "What about the dog?"

If Jimmy says *Dog got*, he is not going to get away with it. Mom will ask for more information: "Did the dog take something? What did the dog do?" *Got ball.* "Whose ball? Your ball? Where did he take it?" (depending on whether mom needs to leap into action and rescue the ball).

These exchanges force Jimmy through the sentence and make him specify what *kind of information* (not which part of speech) is needed and *in what order*. The child's first job in mastering grammar is to understand the rather simple difference between things and actions. As the child gets good at this, more 'brain space' becomes available to contemplate extra details.

The dog got my blue ball.
The dog got my blue ball and ran down the street.

We know that by age two children are well equipped to work out how to say grammatically correct sentences, because they have been able to interpret them for over a year. Children thirteen to twenty months old process every word in a sentence, understand the agent-action-object relationship, and pay attention to function words. In the studies discussed in Chapter 2, infants thirteen to fifteen months could tell the difference between two videos showing a woman kissing some keys or kissing a ball, when asked: "Where is the lady kissing the keys?" Toddlers sixteen to eighteen months old understood who was the *object of an action* ("Big Bird is tickling Cookie Monster") and looked most often at the video that matched the sentence.

At around eighteen to twenty months of age, children showed they relied on function words to help them understand a sentence. When asked to "find the dog for me" by pointing to a picture, the toddlers were nearly 100 percent correct, but they did much worse when *the* was left out altogether ("find dog for me"). And they scored close to chance (just guessing) when *the* was replaced with an unsuitable word or a nonword: "find was dog for me"; "find gub dog for me."

If such young children know all this, why do they speak in two- or three-word sentences? The bottleneck appears to be due to mental efficiency and speech production: how *quickly* they can form a sentence for what they want to say, and how *fluently* they can produce it. My thirteen-month-old took a few days to work out how to say *Go home now Mommy*. It's not easy to carry on a conversation if it takes you one or two days to form a sentence! It's easier just to say the most important words.

Children need two kinds of verbal memory for producing grammatical sentences. The first is memory for simple word order, though this isn't nearly enough. We don't process sentences by their surface structure: The-dog-got-my-blue-ball-and-is-running-down-the-street. We don't remember conversations verbatim; we rephrase them in our own words. Verbatim memory is something only actors have to worry about.

The second kind of verbal memory is syntactic memory, parsing groups of words into phrases: The dog—got—my blue ball—and—is running—down the street. Grouping words into meaningful phrases sharply reduces the memory load both at the processing end and at the execution end. The more this phrase structure of a language has been internalized through listening and practice, the easier it is to remember a novel sentence.

Let's go back to the conversation about the box. This child learned *"take it"* as a phrase, perhaps as a frozen phrase (see Chapter 2). Mothers say: *"Here, take it"* all the time, when they hand the child a spoon, a toy, or a towel. They say it in the present tense as an imperative, almost in the form: [I order you to] *take-it*. In the example, the child's concern was different. She wanted to register a complaint about mom's action in the past, but she knows the verb *take* only in the present tense and only in mom's imperative form *take-it*. That's why it's difficult to impossible to get a child to correct a grammatical error like this one. For the time being 'take-it' is in temporary lock-up. It has been glued together in a phrase.

Morphology and Function Words

WORD ORDER is one part of the problem, but even impeccable word order doesn't get you nearly far enough. If it did, we could say sentences like this one: *I go sleep now Mommy. Get up early, go beach, go swimming?* meaning, "If I go to sleep now, Mommy, then can we get up early to go to the beach and go swimming?" This sentence is ambiguous because the little function words (*to, the, and*) are missing, as are little word fragments (morphemes) that clarify meaning. The function word *to* is missing in its verb form (*to sleep/to go*) and its prepositional form (*to the beach*). The article *the* is missing (*the beach*). The complete sentence implies an if-then construction: *If* I go to sleep early, *then* can we get up early? But, *if*, *and*, and *then* are missing, so the if-then construction is unclear. Also, the question format is incorrect. The phrase *can we*, which would signal a question, is omitted. The listener will know this is a question only if there is a rising pitch at the end of the word *swimming*.

Plugging in all the missing bits would seem like a pretty daunting task, but the average two-year-old polishes this off in about six to nine months. Studies on children's language development show that function words and morphemes tend to appear in sequence, in the same order. However, they don't come in at the same rate, so this clouds the issue. For some children, the rate is so fast, there may be no sequence at all.

Based on average counts for children in the age range twenty to thirty-five months, the common order of appearance of English function words and particles provided in most textbooks is as follows:

PRESENT PARTICIPLES: *ing* as in *swimming*
PREPOSITIONS: *on, in*
IRREGULAR PLURAL: *foot/feet, tooth/teeth*
REGULAR PLURAL: '*s*,' '*z*,' '*ez*' as in *cats, dogs* (dogz),
  and *peaches* (peachez)
IRREGULAR PAST TENSE: *come/came, go/went, grow/grew*
REGULAR PAST TENSE: '*ed*,' '*d*,' '*t*' as in *guarded, seem'd*,
  and *look't*
POSSESSIVE: '*s*,' '*z*' as in *Dick's* car, *John'z* bike
ARTICLES: *the, a*
CONTRACTIONS: *I'll, you'll, it's*

Conjunctions appear when sentence length reaches around five or six words, and when the child is able to link two ideas and make comparisons. The most rudimentary use of *and, then*, or *and then*, is to link elements in a sequence of common routines: *and then—and then—and then*. Here are more sophisticated uses of conjunctions:

and meaning, that's not all, there's more besides:
> "*Sally has lots of balloons, and she has dollies too.*"

but meaning, on the other hand this isn't always the case:
> "*My mommy can bake a cake, but Jane's mommy can't.*"

but meaning, what was intended to happen didn't happen:
> "*I went to Bobby's house, but he wasn't there.*"

If and *because* are causality words and are among the last function words to be used correctly (see Chapter 2).

For some reason, pronouns and future tense verbs, which also appear at this time, were left off the list.

The list indicates different time lines for irregular and regular forms of the plural and past tense verbs. The most common English words are of Anglo-Saxon origin when verbs were irregular, meaning they have no common form. The ten most frequently used English verbs are irregular. These are the verbs children learn first. They are *be/was/were, have/had, do/did, say/said, make/made, go/went, take/took, come/came, see/saw, get/got*. Regular past tense has only one spelling (*ed*), even though it is pronounced three ways as shown above. And there are three pronunciations for plurals as well.

When children begin to use regular verbs and plurals, they sometimes 'over-regularize' verb endings or plurals, mispronouncing words they previously said correctly. This leads to sentences like: *I washed my foots. Mommy goed shopping.* Some linguists believe these errors appear because children acquire 'rules' for past tense and plurals, but there is considerable debate about this. A rule implies a conscious knowledge of linguistic structure. Linguists and grammarians create rules, children do not.

Gary Marcus and Steven Pinker classified hundreds of past tense verbs recorded from spontaneous speech in children ages two to five. Over-regularization turned out to be uncommon even for two-year-olds, occurring only 2 percent to 4 percent of the time, and even this was unpredictable and could change from one sentence to the next: *My daddy went to work. My daddy goed in his car.* More surprising, was that the 2 percent–4 percent rate was constant across the age range, and turned out to be a direct proportion of the number of verbs the child could say. Even adults sometimes slip and make these kinds of errors, especially for infrequently used verbs: *That wind sure blowed last night.*

The message is, that while children make mistakes, they don't do so very often. Nearly all children grow up speaking in grammatically correct sentences. In fact, three-year-olds make grammatical errors less than 10 percent of the time, and by age four, the average child is speaking with nearly perfect grammar.

Questions. Questions.

'WH' QUESTIONS COME in at the same time as function words and word endings. 'Adam' was a child in a famous early study on language development by Roger Brown. Adam, like other two-year-olds, asked lots of questions. Here are some examples of how he handled this as time went by, starting at age two years, four months.

2:4	*See marching bear go?*
2:5	*Where wrench go? What paper clip doing?*
2:6	*What the egg doing?*
2:7	*Where piece a paper go?*
2:8	*How tiger be so healthy and fly like kite?*
2:9	*Where Mommy keep her pocket book?*
2:10	*Do you want a little bit, Cromer?*
2:11	*Do want some pie on your face? Why you mixing*

> baby chocolate? I said why not you coming in?
> Do you want me tie that round?

3:1   You went to Boston University? You want to give
> me some carrots and some beans? Why you put
> the pacifier in his mouth?

3:2   So it can't be cleaned? Do you know the light
> wents off? What happened to the bridge? Can I
> have some sugar? Can I keep the screwdriver just
> like a carpenter keep the screwdriver?
>
> (From Pinker 1994, p. 273)

In the first example, Adam asks a question by making a statement. The only clue this is a question is a rising pitch at the end of the sentence. One month later, he begins using 'wh' question words: *what, where, how, why* (missing are *who* and *when*), plus *do you* and *can I.* He puts these words in the correct slot at the front of the sentence. Notice that *do you—?* is correct at two years, ten months, yet incorrect later on: *Do want some pie . . . ? You want* to give me . . . ? The most notable omissions in Adam's questions are the auxiliary, or 'helping,' verbs that sit just behind 'wh' words, as in *Where **did** the wrench go? What **is** that paper clip doing? What **is** the egg doing? Where **does** Mommy keep her pocket book? Why **are** you mixing baby chocolate?* This construction is inconsistent for Adam until the age of three years, two months.

The Tortoise and the Hare

I WANT TO compare Adam to two-year-old Emily (from Chapter 2) to illustrate the fact that averages for language milestones can be grossly misleading and don't begin to capture the variation in children at this age. Table 1 shows Adam's progression according to the order that particles and function words are supposed to appear in speech. The phrases in the table are from seventy-one of Adam's sentences recorded between the ages two years, three months (2:3) and three years, two months (3:2). Not all the phrases are listed.

TABLE 1.

SEQUENCE OF ACQUISITION OF GRAMMATICAL MARKERS:

Based on seventy-one sentences produced by Adam during one year (Derived from Pinker 1994)

GRAMMATICAL UNIT	AGE	EXAMPLES FOUND
ing	2:4	marching (adj. marching bear)
	2:5	talking, doing
	2:7	going
	2:11	mixing, coming, going
on, in	2:5	put boots on
	2:10	coming in
	3:0	going come in
plural	2:5	boots
	3:0	minutes, mens
	3:1	carrots, beans, peanuts, doggies

GRAMMATICAL UNIT	AGE	EXAMPLES FOUND
past tense	2:6	lost
	2:7	dropped
	2:10	brought
	3:1	went
	3:2	broke, happened
possessive		none
articles	2:3	a bunny-rabbit
	2:4	that busy bulldozer truck
	2:5	that paper clip
	2:6	a piece a paper, that egg
	2:8	the boots, a penguin
	3:0	a baby elephant, those men
contractions	2:6	I don't
	2:10	you don't, I simply don't, I can't
	3:2	I'm going, can't be cleaned, it's got a flat tire, it's need a go, can't come off
conjunctions	2:8	and fly like a kite
	2:11	and tell it
pronouns	2:3	I got horn
	2:6	I lost a shoe, I don't want to
	2:8	let me get down

Grammatical Unit	Age	Examples Found
pronouns	2:9	her pocket book, show you something
	2:10	you don't have paper, do you want a little bit?
future tense verbs	3:0	I'm going come in 14 minutes
	3:0	I'm going to wear that to the wedding

The so-called universal sequence is based on averages, and Adam's remarks don't reflect this sequence at all. He uses *marching* as an adjective quite early. Presumably he has a marching bear, and *marching-bear* may be a frozen phrase. The verb form *ing* appears at 2:5 years. The preposition *on* and the plural *boots* appear in the same month (2:5), but the preposition *in* isn't used until five months later (2:10). Over the year, Adam used six past tense verbs, two regular, and four irregular, and these don't come in any particular order. His speech is notable for the consistent use of the basic present tense form. Interestingly, what is supposed to appear late (articles), comes in early, and Adam used articles consistently from age 2:3 on. Possessives are missing altogether. Contractions appear at age 2:6. There is no fixed progression here, and although seventy-one phrases is a very small sample of the total corpus of Adam's output, it seems that, for Adam, most grammatical forms come in all at once after the age 2:6. Pronouns and future tense verbs were left off the original list—I put them back. Pronouns (*I, me, you, her*) were common in Adam's speech from the beginning (2:3). He never used the future tense, except in the form *going to.*

Table 2 is a breakdown of Emily's bedtime monologue, recorded when she was two years, four months, with tallies for the twenty-nine phrases in this monologue. The table represents only *one point in time,* when Emily was the same age as Adam was at the beginning of his study. At that time, Adam was speaking in two- and three-word sentences: *Play checkers. Big drum. I got horn. See marching bear go. Screw part machine.*

Emily's monologue took place following a conversation with her father at bedtime. He was describing a future event that was to take place that weekend. Apart from hearing her father say *we're going to have a hot dog at the ocean—go to the ocean and have some hot dogs,* the words, sentences, and topics are Emily's own creation, and reflect her concerns and not her father's. Because Emily was talking about a future event, she used no past tense verbs, but numerous future tense verbs appear. The richness of Emily's language, the complexity of the sentences, and the accuracy of the grammar far outstrip Adam's language skills, even when he was three. Yet, by a word count alone, Adam would score high on a measure of spoken vocabulary. Even at the youngest age he used complex words like *checkers, marching, machine, wrench,* and *paper clip.* These examples show that vocabulary isn't all there is to language, and illustrate the profound contribution of grammar to coherent, meaningful speech.

Another unusual feature of Emily's monologue was her use of the verb *think* (*Ocean is a little far away. I think it's couple blocks away*). She used this verb correctly to reflect her mental state. She was trying to work out in her mind where the ocean was, and how to get there. *Think* is fully descriptive of her intended meaning, which is *I'm not sure, but I think this could be true*, stated as a conjecture or hypothesis.

Emily and Adam's language skills are the poles of a continuum. They also reflect the sex difference that is consistent throughout the research on language development. Most two-year-olds fall somewhere between these two extremes.

TABLE 2.
GRAMMATICAL MARKERS
PRESENT AT AGE 2:4:

Based on twenty-nine sentences in a monologue produced by Emily (Derived from Nelson 1998)

GRAMMATICAL UNIT	TOTAL EXAMPLES FOUND
ing	we are going, who's going, I'm going
prepositions	at the ocean, in the ocean, to the ocean, across the ocean, down the river, over by a shore, out to the river, in the river, in a fridge, for the beach, in the red car, in the green car, in my car seat
plural	blocks, hot dogs, car seats, children
past tense	none
possessive	none

GRAMMATICAL UNIT	TOTAL EXAMPLES FOUND
articles	the ocean, a little far away, the river, a fridge, the fridge, a hot dog, the hot dogs, any hot dogs, the water, a shore, the beach, the green car, the red car, the car seats (plus repetitions)
contractions	it's a couple blocks away, it's in, it's downtown, we'll have to go, that's where, who's going to be, I'm going, who's
conjunctions	and across the ocean and down the river, and the fridge, and then we could, and get a hot dog, and bring it . . . and then go, but we could be and we could find, but you know who's going, 'cause that's where the car seats are
pronouns	I think, we could go in, bite me, we go to the ocean, we could be, we could find, we'll have to go
future tense	will be in a fridge, will be in the [water], we'll have to go
auxiliary verb f.t.	we could go in, we could be, we could find

EMILY'S MONOLOGUE:

[we are going] at the ocean. Ocean is a little far away, baw, baw, buh-buh, far away. I think it's couple blocks away. Maybe it's down downtown and across the ocean and down the river, and maybe it's in—. The hot dogs will be in a fridge and the fridge will be in the [water] over by a shore—and then we could go in and get a hot dog and bring it out to the river, and then go in the river and then [?] go in the river and [bite] me —in the ocean. We go to the ocean, and ocean be over by I think a couple of blocks away. But we could be—and we could find any hot dogs. Umm, the hot dogs gonna be for the beach. Then the [fridge?]—We'll have to go in the green car 'cause that's where the car seats are. I can be in the red car, but see I be in the green car, but you know who's going to be in the green car. Both children. I'm going to be in the green car in my car seat. Stephen going to be in the green—.(p. 195)

States of Mind

It is tempting to assume from children's conversations that what they say and how they say it is an accurate reflection of their current mental representation of the world. And while this is true to some extent, this assumption runs into difficulties. We know that children understand a lot more than they can say. From this we can infer that they think in more complex ways than they can express in language. So children's monologues and conversations, while informative, may be on a delayed time line, rather like getting a message that war has broken out in 'Batawongo' six months after the event. Because we can't crawl inside a child's head, it may not be possible to find out what children know, and how they think about what they know, on the basis of how they can *talk* about what they think they know.

There's another possible scenario. It could be that most children think more or less like Emily, trying to imagine how to locate places in space, pondering how to keep the food fresh for a picnic, surmising that the car with the car seats will be the best choice for a trip. Maybe Emily is no more exceptional *mentally* than any other child her age, except for the fact that she can *say* what other children can only think.

No one knows better how to interpret a child's meaning and her mental state than parents do, because only parents know the context and the history behind why a child says what she says. So as I try to put the pieces together and peer into the thoughts of a two-year-old, please keep in mind that this is partly right and partly guesswork.

The questions we need to answer about how children represent events mentally are the same questions asked about the second year of life. How well do two-year-olds remember, what do they remember, and do they have a sense of time past and time future? Are their memories coherent? Do they remember events in sequence? Do two-year-olds remember the story line after hearing a story many times, as parents assume they do? Is a two-year-old aware of other minds? Can she take another person's point of view and see the world from that perspective? Does a two-year-old understand *self* and *other* in terms of how people think and believe? The research on these questions is largely based on what children say and not what they do. Before I discuss this work, I want to return to the fledgling scientists and reflect on how their *behavior* also represents a state of mind.

What Does Behavior Tell Us About How Children Think?

AS A RULE, developmental psychologists believe that two-year-olds (and younger children) live in the moment and don't remember much unless something exceptional takes place (a person touches his forehead to a box and the box lights up). Studies show that children remember routines pretty well (bathtime, mealtime), but apart from this, a child's train of thought prior to age four is decidedly scrappy and disconnected. These conclusions are largely based on the fact that what the child *says* (the only measurement in the studies) is scrappy and disconnected. This belief about children's memory has led to the theory that *language itself* is responsible for locking in memories and making them coherent. I don't think that language is more important in this regard than perception and action. Let's consider for a moment what might have been going on in the minds of the junior scientists.

DOG FOOD

In the dog food example, did Jimmy really feel empathy for the dog, as he seemed to be claiming? Did he really think Robespierre was hungry, and that he fed him because he was hungry, or did this event unfold for quite different reasons? Here's a more likely scenario. Jimmy saw the dog's empty bowl. As he was particularly interested in filling and emptying containers at this point in his life, he decided to fill this one. He got the dry dog food out of the cupboard and poured some in. Mom had left cooking chocolate on the kitchen counter, so that went in. At this point, mom may have come in from gardening to check on him and to get a drink. Jimmy exited from another door to avoid being disturbed. He saw a trowel near where she was gardening, and tossed some wet soil into the mix. Robespierre came up to see what was going on, prompting Jimmy to test out his mixture on the dog.

What is most interesting, should the second scenario be correct, is that Jimmy made up a reason for his actions that had nothing to do with how the situation came about. The reason, *Robey hungy. My feed Robey*, would make Jimmy's action seem not only purposeful, but considerate as well. But we can't know for sure what Jimmy's motive was in saying this. Was he really trying to get himself off the hook (telling a lie), or was he simply describing what he was *doing now*—responding to Robey's evident interest in his dog dish, and letting Robey have a few bites?

Nevertheless, we can make other assumptions, which will be correct. Jimmy remembered where the dog food was kept, and if he could do this, he probably remembered where a lot of other things were kept. Jimmy had a sense that his little experiment might not be appreciated, and he took evasive action. Indeed, secretiveness and evasive action feature in most of the "experiments" outlined earlier.

MECHANICS AND CLOCKS

The language-causes-memory theory doesn't explain a two-year-old's systematic plan for taking four clocks apart and reassembling them over a period of months. How did he remember where the parts went after he removed them without any "clock parts" language? This is not a familiar routine or event. It's a novel and creative act that didn't have to be rehearsed verbally to be remembered. Not only this, but the act evolved into a PLAN, a plan so secret that it was never shared in words with anyone. So secret, in fact, that this child was never caught near a clock, even when he became the prime suspect.

GRAVITY AND FALLING OBJECTS

Here's another purposeful series of novel acts (though *destructive* is probably a better word). Once again, these were carried out systematically on object after object over a period of time. The gravity experiments were also secret events, never discussed or shared, never expanded and made memorable by language. Yet the child's intention was so clear in his mind, that when he was finally caught and asked for reasons, his answer came immediately in a clear, calm voice: *I want to see if this will break*, spoken as if this was the most rational hypothesis in the world.

DISAPPEARANCE

What goes on in children's minds when they try to hide from us in a big, unfamiliar place where we just might go off without them? Hiding is planful behavior, and hiding in a clothes rack is pretty clever. But what is a child *thinking* about as mom and the sales clerk call out his name and run up and down the aisles for about ten minutes?

As the disappearer was my son, I'll continue the story. I decided to try a little experiment before hiding in racks (or anywhere else) became an annoying habit. At around the third disappearance episode, I called to my daughter in a voice a little louder than normal, and said: "We're going now. I guess Geoffrey doesn't want to come with us. We'll have to leave without him." As we walked away, Geoffrey bolted from his hiding place and raced to catch up. I reacted nonchalantly: "Oh, there you are. We were going to leave without you."

Did Geoffrey believe that mothers *always* find little boys who are hiding in racks? Did he even contemplate that he might not be found? Did he have any backup plan for what would happen if he wasn't found? Probably not. Perhaps my remarks framed these possibilities for him for the first time, because disappearance in public places didn't happen after this.

Allyssa McCabe and Carole Peterson recorded a conversation with three-and-a-half-year-old Leah about a hiding episode. This shows that *how mom reacts* has a much stronger impact on what children remember than the reason they were hiding in the first place. The experimenter initiated this exchange:

So you were hiding on your mommy, were you? What happened?

Leah: *Um, ah. She looked in the neighborhood and she looked everywhere. She thought I was killed and she thought a man had stealed me.*

E: Somebody had stealed you. She thought somebody had stealed you?

Leah: *Yeah, but I didn't, 'cause I was hiding that.*

E: You were hiding behind that, were you?

Leah: *'Cause, 'cause I didn't know that she was getting, she said, "Leah get your shorts," and then I was lying down, then, then she couldn't find me. Then that's what, and then, and then, then I came out.* (1991, p. 247)

This was a lengthy conversation, continuing for many more lines. Leah commented again on her mother's reaction: *She gave me a smack on the hand, and she thought that somebody had stealing me—.* (She connects the smack with scaring her mother out of her wits, a good lesson.) Yet in the entire narrative, Leah provides only one vague clue for why she hid: *I thought I was going down the street with M and J—so I wasn't. I was hiding under there.* Apparently she didn't want to go with M and J.

The lesson here is that children's behavior can be quite planful and stealthy, but may arise for different reasons. In the scientific experiments, the rationale is clearly stated, even if it doesn't make sense to us. In the hiding episodes, neither Geoffrey nor Leah seemed to have much idea about *why they hid* or any notion of the consequences of their actions.

Predictable Routines: Marking Time with Words

CHILDREN BEGIN TO USE time words at age two to reflect the connection between events, routines, and parts of the day. They begin to structure relationships between time past, present, and future, with words like *yesterday, today,* and *tomorrow.* These words reflect some notion of cyclical time, time that is revealed through the child's experience of waking and sleeping, darkness and light. What happens after waking is light, followed by breakfast, then lunch, then dinner, then darkness and bed. If other common events are consistently linked with this sequence, they are remembered as well. Time words (*morning, afternoon, night*) help frame these time units and anchor them in memory.

In one of Emily's presleep monologues, when she was nearly three, it was clear she had not only worked out the sequence of daily events, but had some sense of larger time cycles as well, such as days within weeks. She anchored this monologue in real time by using the time word *tomorrow: Tomorrow when we wake up from bed, first me and Daddy and Mommy—eat breakfast, like we usually do* (Nelson 1998, p. 196).

Emily says *like we usually do* (probably one of dad's phrases), which shows she knows this is a highly predictable event. As Emily recounts the sequence of a morning routine in precise order, she links each smaller event in a sequence with *and, then,* or *and then*—meaning next, next, next.

> —**and then** *soon as Daddy comes, Carl's going to come over,* **and then** *we're going to play a little while.* **And then Carl and Emily are both going down the car**—**and** *we're going to ride to nursery school,* **and then** *when we get there, we will say goodbye,* **then** *he's going to work,* **and** *we're going to play at nursery school.* (p. 196)

Next she put nursery school days into a larger time frame, the time frame of one week. This is not just an echo of her parents' remarks, because she does this quite successfully, even though there are no specifics, such as "I go to nursery school on weekdays and stay home on weekends."

> —*sometimes I go to nursery school 'cause it's a nursery school day. Sometimes I stay with Tanta all week. And sometimes we play mom and dad. But usually, sometimes, I, um, go to nursery school.* (p. 196)

Emily hasn't worked out *when* and in what sequence nursery school days alternate with days spent with Tanta (an aunt?) and days spent with mom and dad. But Emily is not oblivious (mindless) of the fact that she *hasn't* worked this out. She used *sometimes* four times. This shows that she knows (remembers) that daily routines change predictably within a larger time frame (a week) but also that she knows she *doesn't know* exactly how and when. She used the words *nursery school day* to mean that a nursery school day isn't every day. She used a causality word (*'cause*), showing that she knows that *particular days* control what she has to do. The fact that it is a nursery school day *causes* her to go there. Nursery school days are not random events. Without these time markers and causality words, the passage would be completely unremarkable: *I go to nursery school. I stay with Tanta. We play mom and dad. I, um, go to nursery school.*

Memory for Past Events

Talking About Past Events Helps Remember Them

PARENTS PLAY AN important role in helping their child make his memories stick so he can find them again. A powerful tool for locking down these memories is reinstating a past event. Not just any event will do. The child has to think the event is interesting or relevant, or you have to *make it* relevant. Discussing a past event is much more likely to lock this event in memory if the child introduces the topic, or at least shows some interest in it.

An equally important element is the parent's style in reconstructing the event. When Susan Engel recorded parent-child conversations with children who were two and a half to three years old, she found that parents tend to come in two flavors. She called these styles "elaborative" and "pragmatic." Elaborative parents set up whole narratives about past experiences with a firm time line, while pragmatic parents repeatedly focus on persons or objects that were central to an event, and use an 'inquisitor' style of questioning. Other scientists, observing the same phenomenon, christened the two types of parents 'elaborative' and 'repetitive,' and these labels have stuck. Here are some examples of these styles in a 'reinstatement' of a past event. The first is an interaction with an elaborative mother.

> *Big cows Mommy.*
>> Cows?
> *The cows come. Did they Mommy?*
>> Oh, you mean the cows we saw on our walk last summer.

Yes, cows last summer.

  We stayed in the little cottage by the beach. We took
  a long walk, didn't we?

Long walk, to a fence.

  Remember we had breakfast, then we walked over
  to the big trees. We walked on a footpath. Do you
  remember the footpath? We had to climb over a
  stile, and you stepped in a puddle.

Yeah. Climb it mysef. Foots all wet.

  Then we walked some more and saw the cows. What
  did you do?

I climb a fence.

  Yes, you got up on the fence, and Daddy held you.
  What did the cows do?

Cows come by me. Cows come over by me and Daddy.

Here is the same event handled by a repetitive mother.

  Do you remember what you saw last summer?

  What?

Last summer, we went to a cottage by the beach.

What did you see?

  Beach.

Yes you saw the beach, but what else? Something big.

  Big beach.

No, not the beach, don't you remember,
you stood on a fence?

  Ummm.

You and Daddy were at the fence. What did you
see at the fence?

  See fence.

What was big and had black and white spots and came
to the fence? Remember, it was a /k/—.

Cow!

Yes, of course, you saw a cow!

Elaborative parents engage in more interactive dialogue, frame the sequences of episodes in descriptive language, and encourage the child to participate while they do this. If the child's feelings and emotional states are connected to these events and reinvoked as well, so much the better. As a consequence, children of elaborative parents remember much more about past events, get the facts straight and in the right sequence, and are able to describe the events in language that is richer and more coherent.

For the repetitive mother in this example, the purpose of the conversation is to get the child to supply the word *cow*. The child doesn't initiate the topic, nor seem very interested in it, and there is little sense that the child remembers this episode (or *will* remember it) as part of an interconnected whole. Repetitive parents' children remember far less and use more impoverished language. The parents question their child repetitively until the child gets the answer the *parent* wants to hear. And if this answer finally appears, parents often don't even acknowledge it or build on the child's input. Instead, they ask more questions. One common observation about this communicative style is that it involves frequent and abrupt shifts of topic. The following example (from McCabe and Peterson, p. 236) is a verbatim conversation between a thirty-month-old boy, Terry, and his dad. (Terry's remarks are in italics.)

[Topic: Boats in the harbor]
    What did we see down in the harbor?
       Boat.
    Yeah.
       (mumbles)

Many?

One boat there.

Which boat?

(mumbles) boat.

[Topic change: Incident where Terry handed his mom a plate of food]

Did you bring supper to Mommy yesterday?

aaaah

Yeah.

Man cook it.

Who did?

Man.

What did he do?

Man cooking supper Mommy.

The man cooked supper for Mommy?

aaah

Oh. And who gave it to her?

Mommy

Who gave the supper to Mommy?

That mom, that mom.

But who brought the supper to her?

(mumbles)

Did you bring it in?

aaah

Did you give supper to Mommy?

aaah

[Topic change: Ducks]

Did you see any ducks this morning?

At this point, Terry began to scream and the tape recorder was turned off.

Terry's perseverance and his willingness to stay in this conversation as long as he did is impressive. Just in case it isn't obvious what dad is doing here, let's analyze this from a 'how not to talk to your child' perspective.

Dad begins by engaging his son on a topic about a visit to the harbor. Terry responds appropriately. Instead of building on this, dad asks him to count the boats. When Terry obliges (*one boat*), he gets no feedback about whether this is right. Instead, he is asked a nonsensical question about "which boat is one boat," a question not even Socrates could answer. As this conversation is obviously going nowhere, dad switches topic. It's understandable that Terry is a poor conversationalist, no doubt from having too many conversations like this one. Here's an example of what dad might have done instead:

What did we see down in the harbor?
> *Boat.*

Yes we did, we saw a lot of boats didn't we? Do you remember, some were big and some were small.
> *Small boat. Bird.*

Oh, you remember the birds! We saw birds sitting on the small boat, didn't we? Looking for fish. Do you remember what kind of birds they were?
> *Fish birds?*

No, they're called seagulls. Can you say seagulls?
> *Seagulls.*

Good! That's very good!

In the real example, dad begins the second topic with a rhetorical question. Knowing that Terry carried a plate of food to his mom, he asks what he already knows: *Did you bring supper to Mommy yesterday?* a sure conversation stopper, because the only answer is "Yes." Presumably that's what Terry meant by *aaah*. His father is then at a loss for words, and says: *Yeah*. At this point, Terry for the first and last time initiates his own topic: "*Man cook it.*" Dad pretends he doesn't understand, and instead of expanding on this, he asks him to repeat what he just said: *Who did? What did he do?* This forces an almost sentence out of Terry, showing his keen interest in this topic: "*Man cooking supper Mommy.*" Dad is now stopped in his tracks and has nothing to say about this, so he repeats what Terry said and gets back to *his* topic: *Who gave supper to Mommy?* It seems as if dad forgot that he knew the answer to this question, because when he began this exchange, he asked: *Did you bring . . .* Dad asks this question four more times, and finally switches the topic to ducks.

Terry wanted something out of this conversation, otherwise he would have run away or screamed much sooner. He clearly wanted to talk to his dad. But the only topic he initiated got him nowhere. Let's look at how dad might have handled this.

> *Man cooking supper Mommy.*
> Well, yes, the man did, didn't he? The man's name is
>   Bill. Bill is a good cook. He made supper for all the
>   people. He made your supper too, didn't he?
> *Yeah, make mine. Hot dog.*
> Did you like your hot dog?
>   Did you like the ice cream too?
> *Yeah. My eat it all up.*

Dad might even want to explore the reason for Terry's interest, such as the fact that women are usually the cooks, not men. *Do you think it's funny to see a man cooking? Mommies usually cook, don't they? But daddies can cook too.* Parents need to think about why children say what they do, *why* they choose a particular topic.

This dad seems to be making a common mistake, believing that what a child can *say* represents all he can understand. He doesn't know that a child who can string four words together in the right order and make sense, will understand a lot. Nor does he know that Terry would be happy *listening* to him talk. Terry doesn't need or want equal time as long as the conversation is remotely related to a topic he's interested in.

Another conversation stopper approach was used by a mother whose repetitive style could be likened to a cross between a parrot and the Inquisition. Each time the child initiated a topic, mom repeated exactly what the child said. When she went into inquisition mode, she didn't rest until she got the right answer, no matter how obscure it was (again, this is from McCabe and Peterson, p. 237).

> Do you remember when we were on the farm at Christmas?
> *I liked Grandpa.*
> You liked Grandpa?
> *Uh-huh.*
> Yea.
> *I love chocolate.*
> You love chocolate?
> [this continues for 12 more lines]
> Who was at the farm when we were there?
> *Umm. Grandpa.*
> Grandpa and who else?
> *Grandma.*
> Grandma and who else?
> *Uncle Bill?*
> Uncle Bill and who else?

This continues through several more people until the child finally named the right person, the person the mother wanted her to name.

These communicative styles don't go away. They continue to be observed in conversations with much older children. One key issue has been whether the parent's style *causes* the child's memory and language skills, or whether it is a *reaction* to the child's input. Teasing this apart has not been easy. If children are matched for vocabulary and basic language skills, and followed over time, the evidence seems to be that the parents' input and style play a causal role in their child's ability to remember and describe past events.

McCabe and Peterson compared mothers' communication styles when their children were twenty-seven months old to the complexity of children's speech when they were three and a half years old. The strongest predictor of the richness of the child's language was the number of statements parents used to extend the topic. The strongest negative predictors were the number of open-ended questions and conversations riddled with topic changes, the conversational style Terry's dad was using.

Regardless of communication style, all studies show that reinstatement, *even if it only happens once*, has a powerful effect on children's memories. Events that aren't reinstated are likely to be forgotten entirely. Further, when memories of events are reinstated by elaborative mothers, children remember much more about them than when they're reinstated by repetitive mothers. Children remember more details and describe the event more coherently, and the quality of their language is better. We'll talk more about how to check your style in the final section of this chapter.

Parents Speak Differently to Boys and Girls

FOR SOME REASON, both mothers and fathers use a more elaborative conversational style with girls and a more repetitive style with boys. In conversations between two-year-olds and their parents, Robyn Fivush found that both parents have longer conversations with girls, ask more questions, and provide more information. Furthermore, girls remembered more about the event than boys. Yet no sex differences were found in basic language skills (vocabulary, grammar) in this group of children. This bias persisted even when the girls showed little enthusiasm for the topic. Instead, parents became even more elaborative, something they did not do with boys. Parents also persist longer in trying to reinstate lost memories in conversations with girls. One possible explanation, which Fivush did not explore, is that there are developmental differences between boys and girls in attention span and behavioral timing.

When my students and I observed preschoolers during free play and recorded exactly what each child did for twenty minutes, we found that boys timed their play differently from girls. They changed activities more often. They were more distractible, responding to sudden or novel events by leaving what they were doing. On average, boys engaged in four and a half activities during twenty minutes; girls engaged in two and a half. The average 'time on task' (continuous focus on the same activity) was twelve minutes for girls, but eight minutes for boys. Boys spontaneously interrupted what they were doing (and returned to it) three times as often as girls. It may be because of boys' greater physical and mental 'fidgetiness' that parents are less likely to engage in elaborative discourse with their sons.

Girls' ability to focus and stay 'in the moment' during conversations with parents means that they will get more information, hear more repetitions of that information, and remember more. Females have higher verbal memory skills across the life span. Girls' verbal memory gets another boost, because parents use more emotion words when they talk to girls, for reasons unknown. People remember more about an event if they had an emotional reaction to it (good or bad). Reinstating emotions about a past event in conversations with children is a terrific tool for enhancing memory.

> Wasn't that a wonderful day!
> Didn't we have a good time!
> He was a very funny clown, wasn't he?
> He made you laugh.
> That ride was a little scary, wasn't it?
> Were you scared?
> What a shame you dropped your ice cream when
> the boy bumped into you. I'll bet that made you sad.
> You cried, didn't you? But Daddy bought you
> another one, and then you were happy.

An elaborative style that focuses on what interests the child and includes statements that extend the topic of interest, and lots of emotion words, lead to more complete memories for past events. There's no reason why parents can't adopt this style if they don't have it already.

It's also true that elaborative conversations about *future* events help children create a mental structure for processing these events, and allow children to experience them more fully. These would include things like going to a friend's home for a barbecue, visiting relatives in a foreign country, taking a trip to the beach, visiting mom or dad's new office, going for a walk in the country, going to a soccer match. Emily's dad should get the prize for effort in this direction. Each night at bedtime, he reviewed what would come to pass in the near future. Of course, he had an ulterior motive: He could get Emily to go to sleep now *in order to* wake up and participate in these exciting events, a great strategy for killing two birds with one stone.

Children's Story Memory

AS WE SAW in Chapter 2, children are ready for the story world in their imagination, sometime toward the end of their second year. Yet young children don't remember much about stories, a fact that only became apparent when children were asked to talk about what they remembered. Parents imagine that young children remember stories like they do, as a coherent sequence of events, especially when they've heard the story dozens of times.

> *Pwease, pwease, Daddy, the fwee pigs!*
> The Three Little Pigs *again?*
> *Yes, fwee pigs. More fwee pigs.*

This is the 2,394th time that dad or mom has read *The Three Little Pigs* to Louise, or at least it seems like it. By now, Louise can even correct errant words or small deletions.

> I'll huff and I'll puff and blow the house down.
> *No, Daddy,* **your** *house down.*

One would expect Louise to whiz through *The Three Little Pigs* verbatim without batting an eye. But, alas, neither Louise nor any other two-year-old can do this. Very few two-year-olds can remember a story line unless the story is very short. And even though they have nailed down particular phrases perfectly, or can link one phrase to the next after a prompt, they have a very hard time telling the story on their own.

One of Emily's most fascinating monologues took place when she was looking through a storybook that her parents had read to her many times. Emily turned the pages one by one, pretending to read, using the appropriate voices for the characters, along with an exaggerated storyteller inflection. She was two years old.

Although the pages were turned in the right order, revealing all those picture prompts, Emily's story-line sequence (based on a true sequence of 1–36) went like this: 27, 31, 34, 24, 3, 1, 3, 30, 18, 24, 27, 36. She began the story at line 27, which must have been a favorite line because she repeats it later on: *I am Dandelion* ("I am Dandelion, he roared"). She got the next two events in the right order: *and it's raining outside* ("It began to rain in torrents"), followed by *it's sunshine out there* ("and the warm sunshine came bearing down"). But these statements were separated by numerous fillers (chat) that had nothing to do with the story: *You better come outside with me. . . . I wanna play with you. . . . Why don't you take nothing? . . . You cannot keep it.*

Seventeen filler remarks followed line 34 before Emily got back to the story to retrieve the event that *preceded* Dandelion roaring: *I am coming to your party, now* ("I've come to your party, he answered"). More fillers followed, and Emily finally got to the opening of the story, but in reverse sequence:

Line 3: *and I know you had a letter.* ("There was a letter—")

Line 1: *I Dandelion woke up* ("On a sunny Saturday morning Dandelion woke up.")

(From Nelson, p. 208)

Emily remembered a lot of detail, but she remembered nothing about *the story*. Children recount stories (but not personal events) as disconnected bits until they're around five years old. Another interesting fact is that if you want to help your child remember stories, it's better to read books with *no pictures*, or to keep pictures out of view. Studies show that young children do a far better job retelling a story that has no illustrations. Illustrations act as memory boosters when they represent something unusual, something the child might not ordinarily know, such as if the main character is a raccoon. Otherwise, illustrations tend to be distracting. They disturb the child's train of thought, and make it hard for her to use her imagination to organize the story. When you think about it, human beings have been *listening* to stories and myths without the benefit of pictures for thousands of years.

Monitoring Other People's Minds

Even babies tune in to other people's emotional states, like happiness, sadness, and anger. It is this tuning in (reactivity, followed by empathy) that allows children to develop an understanding that other people's desires, wishes, and thoughts can be different from their own. The two-year-old who stands defiantly fingering the light cord while staring at mom or dad is monitoring another person's state of mind. This is the same two-year-old who comes in from the garden clutching a dandelion or a petunia and says sweetly: *Fower for you Mommy*. And the same two-year-old who is likely to give mom a hug when she seems tired or sad.

Sometime during the third year, children talk about other people's situations and what might be happening to them, even when this has little or nothing to do with them. When Emily was two and a half, her father had a disappointing experience. Although Emily doesn't identify her father's state of mind with words like *sad* or *upset*, one can sense her genuine concern and her empathy with her dad's situation. Dad had apparently signed on to run in a race, showed up ready to run, and was told he couldn't run. At least this was how Emily construed the situation, which is all that matters. She mused on this that night before going to sleep.

Today Daddy went, trying to get into the race, but the people said no, so he, he has to watch it on television. I don't know why that is, maybe 'cause there's too many people. I think that's why, why he couldn't go in it. So he has to watch it on television.

[She repeats further on:] *But they said no no no. Daddy Daddy Daddy—no, no, no no. Have to watch on television.* (Nelson, p. 198)

Her sensitivity is shown in her use of the words *no* and *has to: the people said no . . . he has to watch it on television . . . they said no no no.* She searches for reasons why daddy couldn't do something he wanted to do. A two-year-old knows the disappointment of *no* and how it feels to be told *you have to* when you don't want to. Emily even conjured up a happy ending, weaving herself into the plot.

But on Halloween Day he can run, run a race. Tomorrow he'll run. He says yes. Hooray! [Emily is invited to join in the race too:] *—a man says "You can run in the footrace," and I said "That's nice of you. I want to!"* (ibid.)

The emotion word *Hooray!* could reflect her sense of what her dad's state of mind *would* be, or her happiness for the changed situation, that is, her happiness for her dad. There is no doubt that Emily is empathizing with her dad's disappointment, because if you strip the dialogue and the emotionally loaded words from Emily's narrative, you would have something like this:

*Today, Daddy went trying to get into the race, but he
didn't. He came back and watched it on television.
Maybe he'll run a race on Halloween Day.*

How well can a child imagine another person's perspective?
Numerous studies have been designed to find out at what age
children become aware that they hold one belief (true belief)
while someone else holds a false belief about the same event. In
a typical experiment, the child and an adult assistant (a stooge
named 'Bob') stand in front of two boxes, one red, one green.
They look inside both boxes. The green one on the right contains
candy, and the red one on the left does not. The stooge leaves the
room for some reason. The candy is switched from the green to
the red box and the lids put back. The child watches the whole
procedure. Then he is asked, "When Bob comes back, which box
will he think the candy is in?" Children up to age four pick the
box *they know* the candy is in.

When the question is presented in this format, children seem
unable to put themselves in someone else's shoes. They don't
appear to understand that while they saw the switch, the person
who left the room did not. However, it turns out that the way
the question is asked, and who plays the part of the stooge, is
critical to whether the child can do the task. If the stooge is a
puppet, and the question is where will he *look?* even two-and-a-
half-year-olds can predict that the puppet will look in the wrong
box. This is an interesting finding. Perhaps two-year-olds have
some vague idea that puppets (toys) don't have minds, and can
be easily confused, whereas human adults can see through walls
and never make mistakes.

This is good news, because it means that two-year-olds have
some notion that story characters have points of view that are
different from their own and other story characters'. Unless the

child can adopt the perspective of one or more of these characters, and imagine how they think and feel as the story unfolds, there won't be as much enjoyment or appreciation (or memory) of the story.

Perspective taking is a product of how parents speak to their children. It is highly likely that Emily's parents made her aware of other people's feelings and desires, and communicated their own feelings and states of mind while events were ongoing. It would be hard to imagine how a child could have this kind of sensitivity, if this wasn't the case.

Preschool: A Word to the Wise

For parents who have the option to stay at home, it is common to start thinking about the pros and cons of preschool when your child turns two. There are numerous studies on the good and bad points of preschool. Not all studies agree. The general consensus is that a good preschool is beneficial and a bad preschool is detrimental. The good versus bad descriptors include such things as quality and training of staff, the number of children in the school, number of children per room, the staff-to-child ratio, the types of toys and educational materials, and how many hours a day the child is there. *Less than 20 hours per week is better* according to a recent study.

I want to say a few words about preschool for parents who have a choice. For the most part, a preschool is not a place where two-year-olds learn what they need at this age, which is lots of one-on-one conversations with familiar people. Nor are all two-year-olds social with their peers. The 'social' reason is the one mothers give most often for deciding to put their child in preschool. A much better reason is to 'give mom a break.' She gets guaranteed free time, which puts her in a better mood, and everyone benefits.

If you're eager to enroll your child in a preschool, here's some advice. Some two-year-olds are too fearful and shy to cope with being dropped in a strange place for several hours. Some are not. Evaluate your child, because a traumatic daily ritual isn't worth it and may turn your child off school. Wait until she's three or older.

Reflect, as well, on how your child reacts when another two-year-old comes to play. Do they sit on opposite sides of the room, silently playing, and totally ignoring one another? Does sweet little Janie sit placidly while her new friend snatches every toy she's playing with? Does David clutch his favorite toys, scream his head off, and refuse to share, prompting his little visitor to bean him on the head with a few loose Legos? Ask yourself if your child will be better off in a room full of little 'friends' like these.

Before you enroll your child, investigate the school thoroughly. How much verbal stimulation will your child receive? Is there a story time or a sharing time? Do the children learn songs and nursery rhymes? Is there a piano or guitar in the room? Are there arts, crafts, or other interesting materials? Is the environment calm and orderly when you drop in?

If you decide to enroll your child, and she settles in happily and seems to do fine, don't leave her there for more than three hours a day, mornings only. This way you can pick her up for lunch, chat about what she did, and give her a nap. (There's no point in paying a preschool for nap time.)

Do keep in mind that without the direct participation of adults, young children don't gain much linguistically from being around children their own age. Two- and three-year-olds are famous for their parallel play and parallel conversations, or interleaved monologues, in which neither party agrees on a topic:

My mommy got a big pumkin.
Look, my picture is red. It's all red right now.

She sez, itsa, itsa halween pumkin.
It's red in the middle. I'm gon make it green
over here.
Did your mommy got a pumkin?
Huh?
A pumkin. Did you got one?
I dunno. Look! I make the teeths green! Ha. Ha.
Pumkin is green, I think.

Unfortunately, there's no substitute for one-on-one conversations to enhance your child's language skills. It's hard to get this kind of one-on-one attention in a day care or a preschool with ten children to every adult. Parents who work and have no choice in the matter, should make the most of their time with their child. Engage her in conversation at mealtimes, bathtimes, riding-in-a-car times, and bedtimes. The good news is that these are precisely the times that your child is in his greatest comfort zone, and most likely to be communicative.

A Parent's Guide

Most of the examples of how parents should interact with their children have been provided in the text. There aren't any hard and fast rules that I can lay out apart from the examples of these good and poor verbal interactions. If you have some concerns about whether you are interacting effectively with your child, then tape several conversations with her, and listen carefully to what you're doing. Here are the major areas of language development that parents influence most. These are also areas where you can monitor your input and do something about it.

Grammar

BECAUSE DIFFERENT LANGUAGES have different grammars, there is no way a child can learn a grammar without your input. There are some useful tips for what works and what does not. But, first and foremost, remember the Golden Rule. Young children need to hear an enormous amount of talk. The more grammatically correct sentences your child hears the better. Try to speak in complete sentences to provide a model. Try not to use too many fragmented phrases or isolated words like these: Gotcha! Wutchadoin? Give Mommy. Some din-din now?

Second, there are some clues about how to fix or shape your child's grammar for the maximum effect. Everyone agrees that it's largely a waste of time to try to correct a child's grammar, to force her to say something in a particular way. This isn't how children learn. There's a better way:

If your child makes a grammatical error, respond to the communication (its intent) using correct grammar. **Don't** try to make your child repeat what he said correctly.

Mommy! Daddy tooked Bartholomew in the car. Did he took him to work? Did Daddy goed to work?
No, Daddy took Bartholomew to the vet. Daddy isn't going to work today. It's Saturday.

Expand on this.

Don't you remember? Bartholomew cut his foot last night. He has to go to the vet. The vet will give him some medicine and make him all better. Daddy will come home soon.

Watch Your Communicative Style

THE SECOND IMPORTANT area is communicative style, something researchers stumbled onto by accident while listening to tapes of parent-child conversations. Parents have different communicative styles, and these styles impact their child's verbal and memory skills for many years. Which of the two main styles, elaborative or repetitive, do you use in conversations with your child? If you're uncertain, or find this too hard to monitor, then record several conversations and listen to what you're doing.

If you sound a lot like Terry's dad or the inquisition mom, you will need to change your perspective about what you believe these conversations are *for*. It's like putting a new frame on an old picture. Instead of using a conversation as a tool to extract a piece of information or a single word from your child (finding out what he *knows*), think of a conversation as a tool for finding out what your child thinks, believes, and is interested in. Here are some useful guidelines for how to accomplish this shift in mind-set:

1. Don't dominate the topic. Let your child talk about what interests her. Follow her lead and keep to this topic until it is exhausted.

2. A conversation is not a teaching exercise in which your child is supposed to prove to you that he knows the precise word or the precise concept you request.

3. Never base your conversation solely on what the child can *say*. Always remember your child understands far more than that. He understands much longer sentences than he can produce.

4. Use your conversation time to find out what he's *interested in*. If you're attentive, your child will give you some clues.

If you ask questions directly related to what the child just said, you'll get more clues. If his eyes light up or he utters a nearly complete sentence (*man cooking supper Mommy*), you'll know you have hit pay dirt. Build on this interest. Put his words or phrase into a longer sentence. Then ask a question about this sentence, or add more information. To find out why Terry was so interested in the *man cooking*, a parent could ask: *Do you think it's funny to see a man cooking?*

5.   Don't forget that your child is interested in hearing *you talk* and is quite happy for you to have more talking time. Just because he is monosyllabic doesn't mean you have to be. But he will still want his turn to respond, so never deprive him of this.

6.   If a monosyllabic word or garbled phrase doesn't make sense (*aaah*), *treat it as if it does.* In the example with Terry, assume that *aaah* is *yes* and act accordingly. This is the only way a child can learn that his utterances have direct consequences. If you ask a question that leads to a yes/no answer, then treat any response as affirmative, unless it is clearly negative, as in *no!*, crying, wiggling, or running away.

Building Your Child's Story Memory

THE GUIDELINES OUTLINED in Chapter 2 on how to build a 'story memory' don't change as the child grows older. If you haven't read that chapter, go back and look at the final section. What you will do differently as the child gets older is to add a little more information in the discussion following the reading of a story. For a young child, one piece of information (who is the main character?) is enough. For older children, two or three pieces of information might be discussed: Who is the main character? Where is she? (location). What is she going to do? (story action).

4.

The Flowering of Discourse

L ANGUAGE DEVELOPMENT FOR THREE- AND FOUR-YEAR-OLDS
is combined in this chapter for two reasons. First, there is
surprisingly little research on language development for this age
group. Second, what research is available shows that three- and
four-year-olds are tackling the same problems, and their progress
is on a continuum. A four-year-old can be considered an
advanced three-year-old, though variation in language development is as great as ever. A large survey on children aged thirty-
six months showed there is a thirty-month age range in spoken
vocabulary. This means that a three-year-old could have the
vocabulary of an average twenty-one-month-old toddler or a
child who's over four years old.

By age three, most children have the full complement of basic
language skills. Much of this year and the next is taken up with
perfecting them. 'Discourse' refers to those language skills that
promote accuracy in communicating intent and meaning, fluency, and richness of expression. Spoken vocabulary increases in
size from around one thousand words at age three, to several
thousand by age four. The average five-year-old can understand
over 10,000 words. But there's a long way to go. People need a

vocabulary of around 50,000 words to carry on normal adult conversations.

A three-year-old is able to monitor his own speech and correct his speech errors. Some children can even reflect on the process. A three-year-old said this: *Nafan is hard to say; it has a /th/ in it.* Grammar improves so rapidly and dramatically, that by age four, it is nearly perfect. Verbal memory improves to the point where children can memorize short poems and nursery rhymes, a major milestone.

Needless to say, parents' input continues to be as critical as ever. Children increase their vocabularies by engaging in conversations, asking and answering questions, and listening to stories. But they decide what to remember, not adults. There are numerous studies on teaching vocabulary in the classroom and in the home. These studies all point to the same conclusion: Direct teaching of vocabulary is largely an exercise in futility. When parents, teachers, and researchers tried to teach new words to children of various ages, it took several hours to achieve only marginal effects (an average of two or three words remembered), with no guarantee the children would ever use them. And while all this was going on, the children were casually picking up around eight to ten new words a day *without conscious reflection or need for practice.* It turns out that children remember the words *they* need for identifying objects and events, and describing the things *they* are interested in. They don't remember words just because adults want them to.

One major difference between three- and four-year-olds is that four-year-olds have a clearer sense of self and an awareness of their own mental processes. It is far easier to explain reasons to a four-year-old. But beware, this doesn't mean that a four-year-old always understands everything you say—far from it.

Denis Donovan and Deborah McIntyre, who specialize in

helping disturbed children and their families, documented this case from their clinical practice. Five-year-old Tom was brought to the clinic for his bizarre behavior and his unruliness in school. A year had passed since his mother died, and Tom was living with his grandmother. She believed she had conveyed the information to Tom that his mother was dead and was now in heaven. But when the therapists probed deeper, they discovered that the child had heard an entirely different message.

When his grandmother told him: "Your mother's gone to heaven," Tom thought that heaven was a place, like the supermarket or the hairdresser's. But wherever she was, she seemed to be taking a very long time. Tom waited patiently for his mother to come back from heaven. Each time he inquired where she was, he got the same answer: "Your mommy's in heaven now." This continued until Tom had been waiting day after day, week after week, month after month, for over a year, for his mother to come back from heaven. Not even an adult could have withstood this kind of uncertainty. When the therapists told Tom calmly and gently that his mother got very sick and died and would not be coming back, Tom's agitation ceased and he began to cry. Not too long after this, Tom was more or less his normal self, and the problem behavior stopped.

This is an example of why it's so important for parents to check on whether their child understands what they *meant* to say. This is especially critical in life or death situations, like the one above. Don't assume a child understands the meaning of life, death, hospital, accident, ambulance, heaven, and so forth.

The Purpose and Function of Language

So far, I have talked more about the nuts and bolts of language, and less about what language is for, or what a child has to learn to use language effectively. Humans are a social species. We live in groups and need contact and communication with one another. Living in groups is complex emotionally, pragmatically, and cognitively. Even herd animals have complex social interactions and intricate communicative signals. If a wild horse doesn't follow 'the rules,' he may be excluded from the herd, at least temporarily. This isolation creates profound fear, one might even say 'loneliness,' and a keen desire to reunite with the herd, a fact that has proven invaluable in developing simple, humane techniques for breaking in a horse to a saddle and rider.

Human infants, like most animal species, come equipped with a repertoire of built-in communicative signals. They cry in hunger, pain, anger, and fear (and each cry is different). They smile, make eye contact, and take turns 'speaking' even before they can babble. They interpret your emotions by the expression on your face and your tone of voice, causing them to feel comforted, fearful, or estranged. They cling, they hug, and want to be hugged back.

By the age of six months, babies know that a particular vocal noise (a word) can stand for something in the world, and from this initial understanding they build a castle called language. I have described the architecture and the construction of the castle, but I haven't talked much about how to use the castle—its purpose and its function. In this chapter I want to stress the *functional* properties of language, which three- and four-year-olds are learning most about, having nearly mastered the structure.

The purpose of language is to convey meaning. Meaning consists of desires, feelings, intentions, information (facts), requests, beliefs, and ideas. All social species communicate meaning about desires, feelings, intentions, and information. Apes and some monkey species have special calls or 'words' for specific predators like eagles and snakes. But only humans share beliefs and ideas with one another. And while human language is the best form of communication we know, it isn't perfect by any means. Human language, like all other communicative systems, is simply a way of *approximating* meaning. If human language was perfect, we could transfer ideas, feelings, thoughts, desires, points of view, *directly*, from one brain to another. That human language falls far short of this ideal is largely the focus of every session of marriage counseling. What Jim means by "spending money" turns out to be quite different from what Joan means by "spending money." What Tom's grandmother meant by "gone to heaven" meant something entirely different to Tom.

Learning to describe and clarify what one really means is the primary linguistic task of the three- and four-year-old child, a task that is never completed. To do this, they need a much better memory. They should be able to remember past events, rely on their memory to pull up the facts, and order them in the correct sequence. They must learn to be consciously aware of the success of their attempts to communicate. They need to monitor how well they're doing, and whether the listener shares common knowledge or needs more information, or needs simpler information. (Most four-year-olds simplify their language when they talk to a two-year-old.) They must learn to stay 'on topic,' and know what *on topic* means. They need to discover that 'parallel conversations' are not conversations, and that neither their peers nor an adult stranger will be nearly as indulgent as their parents in listening to what they want to talk about.

Getting Beyond the Present Moment

Three Types of Communication

MAKING MEANING EXPLICIT, unambiguous, and precise in conversations with family and friends is the primary task from age three on. Initially this effort is vocal (oral). Later on, the same problems apply to written compositions and stories. Research in this area has focused on three types of communication: descriptions of routine events, past events, and the ability to tell a story.

ROUTINES AND SCRIPTS

Routines are familiar, repetitive events within the home, and scripts are familiar routines in the world. The script for a fast-food restaurant is not the same as a script for a proper restaurant. In one case, you get your own food, pay before you eat, carry the food to a table, and bus your own tray. In the other, the food is served to you, you pay after you've eaten, and you leave the dishes on the table. The research question is: How much do children know about common routines and scripts, and how well can they describe them and get the sequence straight?

PAST EPISODES OR EVENTS

Things happen in the past that are not part of any routine. They are isolated events, unlike each other even when they're in the same category. No two camping trips are the same. A child has to learn to remember an event (e.g., a camping trip) as a sequence of smaller events linked by a time line, otherwise his description of this event will be incoherent.

STORIES

To understand a story, or to make one up and tell it to another person, makes more demands on memory and cognitive skill than most three- and four-year-olds can muster. Stories have a unique structure, known as a story grammar. They begin with a flag, which tells the listener that this is a story: *once upon a time, one day*. Characters must be introduced. Some kind of problem occurs that engages the characters. There is a high point in the story, where the problem gets solved, or where the resolution of the problem begins. Another flag signals the story is over (they lived happily ever after). A child who is unaware or unfamiliar with these conventions can't easily oblige an adult who asks, "Can you tell me a story?"

The Development of Narrative Competence

KATHERINE NELSON identified certain abilities she feels are critical in the overall development of narrative competence, underpinning these types. She refers to being a competent listener/interpreter, as well as a competent storyteller and narrator of personal life experiences. Here is an amended version of her list.

1.   The primary aptitude is *language use*, the ability to comprehend and produce connected and coherent speech. This means using correct grammar to signal present, past, or future time, using prepositions and conjunctions appropriately so that precise relationships between actors and events are clear, plus marking which events are causally related.

2.   A second linguistic aptitude is understanding the difference between *necessity*, *probability*, and *uncertainty*. Hansel and Gretel, being led into a dark forest far from home, will of *necessity* be lost. The crumbs Hansel dropped will *probably* lead them home, but because the crumbs were eaten by the birds, it is *uncertain* whether they will ever get there. This sounds very complex and sophisticated, but in Emily's monologues recorded at age two (see Chapters 2 and 3), she frequently made these kinds of distinctions:

Daddy **had to** *watch it on TV* (**necessity**).
Sometimes *I go to nursery school.*
Some days *are nursery school days* (**probability**).
The ocean be over, **I think,** *a couple blocks away.* . . .
maybe *it's downtown* (**uncertainty**).

3. The third aptitude is *memory* for ordering or projecting events in time, plus an *understanding of simple association and causal connections.* If I go upstairs to have a bath, going upstairs does not *cause* me to have a bath, but getting in a tub of water *causes* me to get wet. Two-year-olds can relate the sequence of a highly familiar routine, and may even get the sequence straight, but, as we saw earlier, it takes a long time to sort out causal relationships mentally and be able to represent them accurately in speech.

4. The fourth aptitude is related to the third. Children must have a *firm grasp of routines* and predictable events, in order to be able to 'violate' this predictability and entertain games where boundaries are broken. This begins in fantasy play, something that even eighteen-month-old toddlers happily engage in. Children need to understand that stories are pure fantasy, and that personal narratives are real. This distinction, for some reason, seems to elude children for a very long time (see below).

5. The child must be able to take on the different *perspectives* of the characters in a story, or the perspectives of important people in her life. That children tend to identify with fictional characters suggests these boundaries can get blurred and may not get sorted out until after the age of six.

6. Finally, stories relay *cultural themes and values.* There is no research on how or when these values are picked up by young children. One would imagine they are not, unless they're dis-

cussed and modeled by parents and teachers. Hans Christian Andersen's story about the Dutch boy who held his finger in the dyke and saved the town from flooding, is certainly a model for the cultural values of bravery, selflessness, and steadfastness. But whether young children understand and identify with these themes is unknown.

How well do children accomplish these rather amazing feats of language? We already know that some two-year-olds do a pretty good job with familiar routines: *—and then we have breakfast, and daddy goed in the car, and I play with mommy.* But when do children graduate to being efficient narrators of personal events, and when can they tell a story? Judith Hudson and Lauren Shapiro decided to find out. First, they studied children's ability to provide scripts for common routines, like going to a birthday party, a grocery store, or a restaurant. They found that even two-year-olds have reasonable facility for producing descriptions of these routines. Most of these scripts are in the present tense, and unless the topic is personal (as it is above), the actor in these scripts is the impersonal *you: Well, you get in the car, and then you drive to the grocery store, and you get a cart, and put food in, and you pay the lady.*

This is a typical script of a four-year-old child. It is more advanced than a two-year-old's account, because it contains more propositions (pieces of information), which are more likely to appear in the correct order. The extra information is not a result of having greater knowledge about these routines, but of the child's narrative skill in weaving this knowledge into his descriptions in the right sequence. Other bits of information could just as easily fit into the grocery shopping script, such as *park the car, go inside, stand in line, put the groceries on the counter,* all of which even a two-year-old knows about, but tends to omit.

Hudson and Shapiro set up an interesting format for comparing children who were four, six, and eight years old on their ability to produce scripts, personal narratives, and stories. In each case, the same four topics were used: *birthday party, going to the doctor, Halloween*, and *a trip*. Only the instructions were different:

> To prompt a script, a child was asked, "Can you tell me what happens when you—?"
> For a personal narrative, a child was asked, "Can you tell me what happened one time when you—?"
> For a story, a child was asked, "Can you tell me a make-believe story about—?"

A tally of the number of propositions (pieces of information) used provided an overview of the amount of information children of different ages can impart for scripts, personal events, and stories. The basic findings were these: There was no age difference for scripts, with four- and six-year-olds including five propositions, and eight-year-olds including around six. Four- and six-year-olds did no better with personal narratives, but eight-year-olds managed about fourteen propositions.

The pattern was different for stories. Four-year-olds stayed at the five-proposition level, as if there was some upper memory limit on how many propositions they could string together; six year-olds managed eight, and eight-year-olds, fourteen.

It is puzzling that the number of propositions used in scripts didn't vary across this rather large age range. Children may perceive this as a hollow exercise, because they're well aware that adults know all about these familiar routines. In fact, three-year-olds produce more incoherent and vague accounts of a personal event when they tell it to a familiar adult than when they tell it to a stranger, showing they take the knowledge of the listener into account.

As a count of propositions alone doesn't reveal the characteristics of the narratives of the three age groups, the children's narratives were broken down further into various structural elements. These are listed separately for each type of narrative.

SCRIPTS

Similarities were found between all age groups in the use of the present tense (80 percent of the children) and the pronoun *you* (about 50 percent of the children). Of the remaining structural elements, four-year-olds were notable for having extreme difficulty getting the sequence straight—only 20 percent were successful at this. In addition, only 20 percent added optional or qualifying remarks, like *usually* and *sometimes*, whereas this was common for the older children.

PERSONAL EVENTS

Nearly everyone used the past tense and first person pronouns (*I went to the circus*). Surprisingly, the four- and six-year-old children were virtually indistinguishable in their use of other structural elements, but quite different from the eight-year-olds' use. They were far less likely to provide a setting or any background information. Only about 40 percent got the sequence straight, and few provided an ending. Typical narratives of the four-year-olds are shown in the following examples (from Hudson and Shapiro 1991, pp. 132–36). The instructions were 'Can you tell me what happened one time when you—' followed by one of these four phrases: 1) had a birthday, 2) went to the doctor's office, 3) went out on Halloween, 4) went on a trip.

*Well there was a cake. And there were people and pres-
ents and cards on the present. And there was candles on
the cake. And they light. And we sing Happy Birthday.*

I got a shot. I didn't cry though. Then I went home.

*Well, me and my mommy, and we went outside for
Halloween. And I remember that I was a fairy princess.
And I got a lot of stuff in my bag. And I remember
my sister was a clown. And we went to some houses
with my mommy to get a lot of stuff together. And
that's all I remember.*

*We went on a hike and we saw turtles on a log. We saw
alligators. We saw fish. We saw birds and birds' houses
and holes in the ground that squirrels lived in. And then
we had a picnic. And then we went home.*

STORIES

Age had the largest impact on how children managed the
storytelling exercise. Nearly everyone used the past tense, but only
eight-year-olds had a good grasp of the structural elements that
make up a story. Four-year-olds were at an extreme disadvantage
in this task. Only 40 percent of the four-year-olds succeeded in getting events in some kind of sequence, the same proportion found
for personal narratives. But that was about all they could do. Few
four-year-olds provided a setting or any fictional characters. Less
than 33 percent included any problem or surprise to make the story
interesting. Almost no one provided a resolution or an ending.

Only two stories from all age groups were about fictional
characters (animals), and only one of them had a plot.
Surprisingly, by far the best story came from a four-year-old:

> *Once there was an ostrich and he couldn't fly but he walked all the way to Florida. And then he found it was too hot there so he went back to here and it was too cold. He just stayed here thinking of where he could go where it wasn't too hot and it wasn't too cold. Then he just said: "Let's stay here."*

Of course, this might be borrowed from a familiar children's story, but, even so, it was the only example where the child was able to follow the directions, and knew what a story was.

Despite the large age differences, there was something the children did share in common, regardless of age. Nearly every story was about the child who told it and was delivered in first-person pronouns (*I, me, my*). This was even true of half the stories told by eight-year-olds. Most children interpreted the phrase "make-believe story" as something resembling a fantasy, similar to pretend play, as seen in these examples:

> *Well, I pretend that one of my friends—*

> *You can make pretend you have a car.*

It seems that children don't understand the nature or the structure of a story, and they tend to integrate fairy tales and fictional stories into their own lives, identifying with one of the characters. One five-year-old in another study believed that he and Peter Rabbit were essentially the same person. This might explain why, when young children are asked to tell a story, they don't bother with fictional characters but create a story about themselves.

Even when children come to understand that story characters aren't actually themselves, many still believe the events and the characters in the stories are *real*. One study showed that half of the six-year-olds interviewed about well-known story characters thought the fictional characters were real, and, if not alive at the moment, had lived some time before. One six-year-old stated that while Cinderella was not alive today, she was alive *"a long time ago, when I was one years old."*

These findings raise a number of thorny questions for parents. What purpose is served by reading fictional stories to a child? All the evidence shows that children can't remember the story line, the plot, the rationale, or the theme until they're six to eight years old. Is it a good idea, or is it unhealthy and dangerous, to identify too closely with a fictional character? Does it really matter whether a child can tell a story or not? I'll try to answer these questions further on. However, there are principles everyone can agree on: Children should tell the truth, remember important facts, and be able to describe past events accurately and thoroughly. *Children need to learn the difference between reality and fantasy.*

How Parents Help Children Improve Memory and Language

Remember the elaborative parents discussed in Chapter 3? They engage in more interactive dialogue, frame the sequences of episodes in descriptive language, and encourage the child to participate while they do this. Repetitive parents, on the other hand, use impoverished language and question their child repetitively about some fact or facts until the child gets the right answer, that is, the one the *parent* wants to hear. In Chapter 3 we saw how these types of parents interacted with their two-year-olds. Perhaps repetitive parents have a poor communicative style because their children don't say much, and the conversation falters. If this is the case, then one would expect the parents' style to change noticeably as their children grow older and develop better language skills.

Conversations between mothers and their three-year-olds were recorded by E. Reese, who followed up with the children when they were six. The children were initially matched for language ability and split into groups depending on their mother's communicative style. Amazingly, the repetitive parents' 'inquisitor mode' of interaction changed relatively little over this long time period. Though these parents did become slightly more elaborative when their children were six. They would have to; no one can carry on a normal conversation in this mode. When the children were given language and memory tests at age six, there were large differences in memory and language skills between the children with the two types of mothers. The children with elaborative mothers remembered much more about past events. Their language was richer, better organized, included more detail, and contained more comments related to personal involvement or perspectives.

This type of study is known as a 'descriptive study,' one where conversations are recorded as they spontaneously unfold. Another way to study the same phenomenon, and to estimate the importance of a mother's verbal style (rather than some other contributing factor, like verbal IQ), is to set up an experiment. Minda Tessler and Katherine Nelson had mothers take their three-and-a-half-year-olds to the natural history museum. Half the mothers were told to discuss the exhibits with their children as they normally would do. The other half were told to say nothing unless the child asked a question, in which case they were to answer it correctly and succinctly. The children whose mothers chatted about the exhibits in the normal manner remembered far more about the experience one week later.

But Tessler and Nelson found something else. Prior to this study, they knew nothing about these mothers. However, the museum conversations were taped, and when the researchers listened to them, they were struck by the different styles of interaction among the mothers who were asked to talk 'normally' to their children. It was easy to distinguish the elaborative or repetitive types. What was significant about the elaborative mothers' style was their frequent use of analogy, the attempt to make a connection between what the child was looking at and his past experience. When their children were compared with the children of repetitive mothers, the children with elaborative mothers had far better recollections of this experience. So it is not only beneficial for parents to *enlarge* on what children notice or talk about, but also to make connections between things present and things past. Making analogies is one of the important aspects of the highly effective communicative style, 'symbolic emphasis,' that Hart and Risley documented (see Chapter 1).

The researchers made another remarkable discovery. The child's ability to remember the exhibits in the museum was largely a function of whether there was a *mutual conversation* about them. If the child made a comment and the mother failed to respond, or the mother made a comment and the child failed to respond, *the child remembered nothing* about that particular exhibit. This is an important finding, because it shows that mutual attention and *shared experience* (communication) plays a major role in whether children remember past events at this age, or at least remember them well enough to put their images and thoughts into words.

A similar type of study was done with four-year-olds who accompanied their mothers on a photography outing. In this study, the mother's communicative style was identified ahead of time. Mother and child were told to cooperate in selecting items to photograph and in taking the pictures. The researchers kept the film and had it developed. Each child was interviewed in his home and shown the pictures for the first time. The interview style varied. The researchers prompted the children with either an elaborative question (*Why did you take this picture? What were you trying to do here?*) or a repetitive question (*What's this?*) They thought the child would be more likely to respond in kind, regardless of their mother's communicative style—but that didn't happen.

Mom's style is highly contagious. Children who had elaborative mothers were elaborative talkers, and answered elaboratively anyway, and children who had repetitive mothers were consistently concrete and monosyllabic. Here are examples of the kind of statements each type of child would make to a question framed in the repetitive mode: "What is that?"

Child of elaborative mother: *Um, well this is an old church. Mom liked it a lot, but she let me take this one. I wanted to, um, not get that building in it, but it didn't come out right did it? It's crooked isn't it?*

Child of repetitive mother: *It's a church.*

Reinstatement of past events, talk about future events, and interactive conversations about ongoing events contribute equally and impressively to whether children remember those events and can talk about them coherently. Not only this, but the parents' conversation style has a profound impact well beyond this. Can this knowledge help parents (and teachers) do a better job helping children understand the story world?

Interpreting the Story World

IN THE MARKET SQUARE in Marrakesh, even today, a story-teller sits in the dirt with a tattered book, reading aloud to young men and boys who listen with rapt attention. Everyone loves listening to stories, even children as young as one year old, who can't understand most of the words.

Children's stories resemble the fantasy world that they introduce into their play at around eighteen months. This is a world where animals can talk, ride a jet ski, and drive cars. Yet while children seem to know their fantasy play is 'just pretend,' they aren't nearly so sure about stories. Adult readers may identify with a character in a novel, but what about the child who thinks he's Peter Rabbit, or believes Winnie the Pooh is real? Should a child populate his inner world with fantasy characters like Santa Claus and the Easter Bunny?

Humans by nature are magical thinkers, and because of the way the brain works, we have a tendency to make causal connections between events that co-occur. This results in things like interpreting rare events as prophesy: I knew that when the clock stopped at that time, it was a sign. Children often indulge in magical thinking. Yet magical thinking is something that education is supposed to get rid of. So where do we draw the line between fantasy and reality? Children who think too magically sometimes imagine they can jump off the roof and fly. Little girls who read *Cinderella* are convinced they too will be asked to a ball by a prince.

But if too much 'fantastic' is not a good idea, it is also true that 'super realism' doesn't warm many hearts. No child is more likely to be friendless than the kindergartner who regales her classmates with the logical arguments for why Santa Claus could not possibly deliver toys to all the children in the world in one night. We have a soft spot for poetic Ernie who says the moon follows him around, but feel decidedly uncomfortable with Arthur who tells us that the moon is a giant piece of rock millions of miles away that orbits the earth.

How do stories help develop children's knowledge of the world? Do they, in fact, help children develop better language skills, firmer ethical principles, and an awareness of cultural values, as educators claim? Does a child really acquire these attributes by listening to children's stories and fairy tales written in eighteenth- and nineteenth-century Europe? Wouldn't she be better off having a discussion of real events with family and friends? I don't have the answers to these questions, but I can share my biases. I vote that stories are good for kids. We certainly know that stories help build vocabulary. One study showed that children's literature contains more complex words than adult sitcoms on TV and college students' conversations. But parents can make better use of story time by insuring that children get the most from them. By this I mean understanding the nature of a story, insuring a reasonable grasp of a story grammar, helping the child be aware that all stories have a similar structure even though they are about vastly different things, and that a story is not a script or a personal narrative. Parents can help sort the world of make-believe from the world as it really is. None of this can be explained directly to a child, but parents can highlight story elements as described earlier, preferably *after* they read the story through uninterrupted at least once. Then they can begin to ask the following kinds of questions at about the rate of one per reading.

> **Setting:** Do you know where this is? Is that a real place?
> Can people really live at the bottom of the ocean?

Characters: There are a lot of animals in this story. What are their names? Do you know what kind of animal that is? Can a giraffe really talk?

Plot: What do you think they're doing here? Let's read this part again. Why are they doing that? Do you remember what happens next?

High point: Did you think the animals would be safe? Did you think they would get to go home? This was a pretty exciting story wasn't it?

Ending: What did you think of the ending? Everyone was safe/happy/home again, weren't they? Did you like this story? Did you think Sam was brave/silly/clever/lazy? Did this really happen? It's just make-believe, isn't it?

Some Old Unsolved Problems

> *Mummy, I always ask why. Why do I always ask why?*
> Because you are curious about things.
> *What is curious?*
> —three-year-old recorded by Callanan and Oakes, 1992

Causality and Time

KEEPING THE SEQUENCE of a personal narrative straight and remembering a story line have to do with understanding causal connections and temporal progression. Three- and four-year-olds are still struggling with the problem of causality, not only how to express it in words, but also understanding causality in the world. Maureen Callanan and Lisa Oakes studied the kinds of questions preschoolers ask when they are three, four, and five years old. Mothers kept a diary for two weeks, and recorded every question their children asked and how they responded to it.

The age of the child made little difference to the number of questions asked, the type or form the question took, or the complexity of the conversation that followed. 'Why' questions were asked most frequently, followed by 'how' questions. But the child's age did make a difference in what the child wanted to know about. Three-year-olds were most interested in reasons (motivations) for behaviors, followed by physical mechanisms or how things worked. Four-year-olds were interested equally in motivations, physical mechanisms, and biological phenomena. Five-year-olds were interested in motivations, biological phenomena, and cultural conventions, in that order, indicating that they were becoming more socially aware due to their being in school.

Mothers' responses to these questions depended on the age of the child, particularly for 'why' questions. 'Why' questions (*Why do you hang the clothes outside?*) led to three types of causal answers, *prior cause* (because the sun dries the clothes), *consequence* (we can't wear wet clothes), or *both*. Mothers' responses to three-year-olds were more likely to be noncausal, stating a fact: to dry them. Responses to older children were more likely to be causal, and the older the child, the more complex the causal answers became. It is interesting, once again, to see how well mothers spontaneously tune their response to their child's age and understanding.

Surprisingly, these spontaneous question-answer sessions rarely occurred during play sessions with mom. Instead, they popped up during familiar routines, such as bathtime, bedtime, meals, riding in the car, and even watching TV. These five settings accounted for 88 percent of all questions asked by the children. As noted in the previous chapter, these are the settings where children feel most at ease and aren't too preoccupied or distracted. This is useful information for working mothers who often have *only* these times with their children.

Preschool children are obviously keen to figure out how the world works, and they are still struggling with making sense of time, an essential ingredient for a true understanding of causality. In Chapter 2, I provided a list of time words that parents use as a matter of course. By age three, children use these time words as well, but without understanding much about what they mean.

One of the biggest puzzles that three- and four-year-olds have to solve is cyclical time and nested time (sequences of routines within days, days within weeks, weeks within months). Two-year-old Emily tried to figure out how 'nursery school days' fit into a larger time unit (week), which did *not* always contain nursery school days (she was unsuccessful, I might add). In the example below, three-year-old Steven tackled a similar problem on his walk to preschool.

> Steven: *This—remember the water was here—the old puddle was here when it rained tonight?*
> Mother: When it rained the other day.
> S. *No, it rained yesterday.*
> M. No, it rained the day before yesterday.
> S. *No, it was the day before—yesterday. It was now yesterday!*
> M. It was now yesterday??
> S. *No, when we were—when it was night then— nighttime then it was yesterday. When we waked up— when we had some supper—then we went to bed, then it was nighttime, then the sun was out, then it was night- time, then it rained, then we waked up, then we, then we goed, then we went in that puddle.* (Nelson 1998, p. 272)

Steven is struggling with the thorny problem that yesterday (like tomorrow) can never be today. He seems to recognize this problem and begins backtracking to reconstruct the day before yesterday. He does something fascinating. When he tries to go backwards by yesterdays, he only succeeds in going *forward* by events within days, starting with supper—then bed (night-time)—then sun comes up—then night—*then it rained*—then it's the next morning (today), the day they went in the puddle. This gets him back where he started, but in a worse mess than before, because today (the real today) is now the day they went in the puddle, instead of the day before yesterday! That a three-year-old can attempt this mental feat is remarkable. And it surprises us, because preschool children are utter dunces about clock time. Many children believe the clock stops while they are sleeping.

My Topic or Yours?

AT SOME POINT, young children must become sensitive to their conversational partners. As we have seen, parents have greater success in conversations with their children when they follow the *child's* lead, and expand on a topic the *child* introduces or is interested in. But this is a one-way street, and children won't get along with their peers if they continue to expect this kind of indulgence.

In the example of parallel conversations in the previous chapter, we saw that two-year-olds don't make much progress in settling on a mutually agreed upon topic. In the example there was a conflict of contexts. One child was relating information about an experience at home (out of sight) and the sudden appearance of a pumpkin, while the other child was putting her current actions into words. Young children's conversations work best during mutual play, and the more familiar the context, the better. Success is greater when they chat about common knowledge, like making dinner in the playhouse or building cars with Legos. Conversations improve in new activities as well, *if* children are doing the same thing or cooperating, like stringing beads, drawing pictures, or building a tower with blocks.

Nevertheless, the ability to carry on a conversation with a relative stranger is not an easy task, as everyone knows. Some people are much better at it than others. Nelson recorded this extraordinary conversation between two four-year-old girls at a preschool. I should point out that girls are usually better conversationalists than boys.

    A. At morning it's lunchtime.
    B. *But first come snack, then comes lunch.*
    A. Right—Just in school, right?
    B. *Yeah, right, just in school.*
    A. Not at home.
    B. *Well, sometimes we have snacks at home.*
    A. Sometimes.
    B. *Because when special children come to visit us, we sometimes have snack. Like, like, hot dogs, or crackers, or cookies or, or something like that.*
    A. Yeah, something. Maybe cake.
    B. *Or maybe hot dog.*
    A. Maybe hot dog.
    B. *But, but, but, Jill and Michael don't like hot dog. Don't you know—but do you know Michael and Jill?*
    A. I know another Michael.
    B. *I know. I know another Michael.*
    A. No, I know just one Michael. I just know one Michael. (p. 148)

What is remarkable about this exchange is not so much that the children stay on the same topic, but that they can switch contexts from school to home to people they know, without losing the thread of the conversation. They are able to adopt different frames of reference and then add to them. Child B could even take the perspective of the listener, realizing she might not know the same Michael. I suspect these children have elaborative mothers and fathers. This kind of conversational skill, in which these young girls affirmed what the speaker just said then expanded on it, has to be modeled; it doesn't spring into being overnight. There is no developmental rule that all children magically become good conversational partners simply because they get older. Many adults make abrupt changes in topic or fail to take the listener's knowledge into account. In recordings of children across a wide age span, these kinds of conversational errors are common, even among teenagers.

Topic shifts can become a tool. Married couples are expert at the topic switch technique to avoid having to discuss something unpleasant.

> Marcia: *I need to talk to you about something.*
> Jim: Have you seen my green striped tie?

> Frank: *About those credit card bills—*
> Sue: Did I tell you that Jennifer got on the track team?

Harold Pinter writes entire plays with this kind of dialogue.

If you want to encourage your child to be a good conversationalist (and a good writer), you need to model the elaborative style if you aren't already using it. Once your child gains some expertise and fluency, begin to signal when she hasn't made something clear: "*Which* Michael at school? Don't you know two Michaels?" This is a good way to sensitize your child to the fact that the listener can't always be expected to understand what you mean, and that you may be inferring knowledge your listener doesn't share. This has excellent spin-off for developing good writing skills, and mastering the difficult task of holding the reader in mind as you write.

More About Preschool

Children can't become good conversationalists with their peers unless they have some peers to talk to. If you live in a safe neighborhood where lots of children of different ages play together, then a preschool experience isn't that relevant. If you live in an apartment building, a busy city, or remote country village, preschool is probably a good idea.

Keep in mind that at this age (but not at two), the primary benefit is social: learning how to interact appropriately with peers, to share toys and space, to engage in mutual play, and to be able to carry on sustained conversations where both parties stay on topic. Other benefits could include getting used to being in an unfamiliar environment, learning to interact with strange adults, and learning to respect and follow rules that benefit the group. There should also be some exposure to art and music. Plus, a good preschool will have far more equipment and materials than most homes can provide.

Be aware that, apart from peer interactions, a preschool experience will not benefit language (or literacy) in any significant way. Adult-child conversations occur far less frequently in preschool than in the home and tend to be shorter when they do. This is a function of logistics. Children outnumber staff by around ten to one, and a major portion of the teacher's time is taken up maintaining order and enforcing rules.

David Dickenson found, during many hours of observations in a well-run preschool, that when teachers circulate around the room, supervise play outside, or sit at the lunch table, most of their talk has to do with enforcing rules and managing behavior. The few one-on-one conversations with individual children took place when the teacher was stationary and not on duty, seated at the crafts table, for instance. Teachers, like parents, had the same differences in conversational style. Some teachers drew children out, made jokes, reinforced and affirmed what the child said, and were enthusiastic. Others were more didactic, and their agenda was paramount; they repetitively questioned the child about something like naming a letter or supplying the correct word for an object.

It's easy to see why children aren't likely to gain much from an interaction with adults in a preschool setting. The question about whether children learn conversational skills in interactions with peers has received little attention from researchers. The sophisticated conversation between the four-year-old girls presented above is not typical. (Researchers tend to publish the most extreme examples of the many examples they collect.) Whether it's necessary for three- and four-year-olds to talk to each other for normal social and language development, or whether preschool fosters this development above any other type of social setting, is unknown.

Other studies have shown that children in preschool settings tend to be less curious and engage in less complex or cognitively demanding tasks. During free play, some children return again and again to the same activity. In Montessori preschools, which are probably the best preschools around, teachers joke about weaning a child off a favored activity, like spooning water from one container to another. In my preschool study (see Chapter 5), the observers got the strong impression that the preschool environment was overwhelming for many boys, especially boys who are sensitive to novel visual stimulation. The greater distractibility among boys (frequent switching between activities, high number of interruptions of ongoing play) seemed to be as much a function of the environment as of the child. I hasten to add that this type of behavior is far less common in Montessori schools, which are notable for their order and tranquility.

A Parent's Guide

This chapter presented several discoveries about the impact of parents' verbal style on children's memory skills. For one thing, we know that trying to teach new words because *you* have chosen them won't work. Children's spoken vocabularies increase at an amazingly rapid pace, but consist of words *they* want to know, for what *they* want to say. These are usually words the child has heard many times before, and repetition seems to be important. The difference is that the words the child learns to say have been heard in various contexts at different times, not in some repetitive drill.

How to Encourage Vocabulary Growth

THERE ARE MANY other ways to contribute to your child's spoken vocabulary. Children learn more words if parents gradually increase the complexity of their remarks; this means more new words, longer words, and longer sentences. Try it out. If what you say is too complicated, you'll hear about it. If you're not sure, then ask: *Did you understand what I just said? What didn't you understand?* Children learn new words to go with new experiences, new places, new things. Going to the science museum or the exploratorium is a great way to teach new vocabulary (think about how easily young children master complex Latin names for extinct reptiles). Children remember and use new words that relate to something they observe or are interested in. If your child asks you for a name, use this opportunity to expand on his interest and tell him a little more than he asked for, repeating the word over and over: *Oh, that's a beetle. Beetles won't hurt you at all. Beetles have six legs. See?* If your child has developed a passionate interest in something, like dogs for example, you can start naming breeds (the subordinate category words). *That black and white spotty dog is a dalmatian.*

CHECK IT OUT

How well does your child manage routines and scripts? How well does she do if you ask her to tell a story? Here are some simple games to find out.

In a play situation with your child, choose one of her floppy toys or a hand puppet, preferably one with a silly smile on its face. Start a little conversation about how this toy (let's call him Mumbo) doesn't know very much. He just lives in the house and doesn't go to school, to church, or to the grocery store. Perhaps your child can tell him about what you do at the grocery store. If you have a hand puppet, start the game this way:

> Mumbo, do you know what a grocery store is?
> *[Mumbo shakes his head.]* Oh, look, Mumbo
> doesn't know what a grocery store is. He never
> went shopping for food with us, did he? Why don't
> you tell him what we do in the grocery store?
> Would you like that Mumbo? *[Mumbo nods.]*

If you want to keep a record, count up how many propositions (pieces of information) your child produced for the grocery store script. Notice if they came in the right order.

STORY GRAMMARS

Despite the fact that children hear thousands of hours of stories, remembering the story events in the right order and being able to tell a story from scratch is incredibly difficult until children are at least eight years old. One problem is a lack of awareness of a story grammar. One might imagine that anyone could extract a story grammar just by listening to stories, but they can't. Perhaps you didn't know there was such a thing as a story grammar until you read this book. Yet we know this grammar is as important for organizing memories of the story content (telling a familiar story), as it is for organizing how to tell a novel story.

Jill Fitzgerald and Alan Teasley developed a program for teaching a story grammar to nine-year-olds to improve their written work. These children were compared to another group of children who spent the same amount of time reading stories and looking up words in the dictionary. The children were asked to write stories after the training ended. Those trained on a story grammar had much higher scores on story organization, story quality and coherence, and creativity.

There's no need to wait until your child is nine years old to get the benefit of this type of training. You can start to play a storytelling game with your child beginning at age three, one where you and your child take turns telling stories. Make this part of a bedtime routine or some other routine. It is easier to teach one story feature at a time. To make this more gamelike, be as outrageous as you like with your story. Start the game by saying: *I'll tell you a story, if you tell me one.*

STORY BEGINNINGS

Focus first on story beginnings. Stories usually begin with a flag to signal that this is a story, and this is the *beginning* of the story ("Once upon a time"), though this isn't essential. Next, you want to describe a *setting* and introduce one or more *characters*.

> A long, long time ago, there was a little boy who lived on a tall mountain that had lots of donut trees and apple juice waterfalls. The little boy was four years old, and had big, blue eyes and red hair.

Make up whatever story you want. If your child is unfamiliar with anything in the opening, then describe or explain it, or draw him a picture. If he wants more information, give it to him, but make sure it relates only to this part of the story.

Then say:

> How do you like this story so far? This is how my story begins. Now it's your turn to tell a story beginning. You have to think of something different. You can't use my story. [*Refuse to continue your story until your child has taken his turn.*]

Depending on how he gets on with his story, orient him to what information comes first, and if he leaves something out, then ask for more information:

Where does this story happen? Where is that?
What kind of place is it? Who is in this story?
What does he look like? Is he old or young?
Is this an animal or a person?

Children often use themselves as the main character, as we saw earlier. Tell him he can't be the main person in his story, nor can anyone else he knows. The main person has to be made up. That's the rule in this game. After you sort this through, write down the child's final solution. (Write down your own story as well so you can remember it.) You can continue this effort, or save the next step for another day.

OTHER STORY FEATURES

When you come back to the story the next night, follow the same pattern with each story feature (one at a time) in sequence. The next story feature is the *plot*. Break down the plot into two components and deal with each one separately.

1. A precipitating event. This can come about due to action on the part of the main character, or something that happens to the character from outside. This event can lead to a novel experience, a challenge, an obstacle, anything that initiates action.

2. The reaction of the protagonist or opponent to this precipitating event. This could include planning, plotting, fleeing, fighting, hiding, or any type of action.

After the plot (the action component) plays itself out, the next story feature is the *story resolution*, the high point where the problem is solved, the journey ended, and so forth, and everything returns to normal, or there is some life-changing event (people get married). Finally, there is another flag known as the story *ending*: *They lived happily ever after and never saw the wicked dragon again.* If your child really likes this story game, and her brothers and sisters do too, you can continue to play it for years.

In next chapter, I take up the topic of reading instruction: how to acquire the skills to read stories and to write them. If parents have followed the suggestions in this book, their children should have all the necessary language skills to be a good reader and writer. What the child needs next is how to master the code for turning speech into written symbols and back again.

5. *All About Reading*

U P TO THIS POINT, YOU HAVE LEARNED MANY WAYS TO enhance your child's language development. A child with good language skills is on the way to becoming a highly literate adult, in the true meaning of the term. This child has a rich vocabulary and understands the words she reads; she can grasp the subtleties and nuances of sentence structure and meaning. This is the child who is familiar with written genres: the many forms of written compositions—narratives, nonfiction, poetry, and stories.

One hurdle remains—learning to read and write—the ability to *decipher the code* that gets us from spoken to written language and back again. In the best of all possible worlds, this book would end here. Your child would go to school; well-trained teachers would take over and, using the latest foolproof methods, teach every child to read in a year or less. After all, this is what schools were created for. If children didn't have to learn a writing system or a number system, we wouldn't need schools. The goal of universal education was to insure that *all children* learned to read, write, spell, regardless of their background and circumstances. Sadly, that goal has not been fulfilled for all children in English-speaking countries.

Most parents are justifiably concerned that their children may not learn to read, and many begin to teach their children before they start school. But parents, like most teachers, aren't properly trained in how to teach reading. This chapter provides a crash course on how our writing system works, discusses why the schools have failed in their primary task, and offers clear guidelines for what you can do to ensure that your child learns to read, write, and spell accurately and efficiently.

There are many reasons why ineffective methods of reading instruction are the norm rather than the exception in classrooms around the English-speaking world. One is due to our opaque (unpredictable) spelling system. Other reasons are historical, financial, and political. And there is the inertia that sets in once invalid methods are in place. These reasons are discussed fully in my two other books (please see Suggestions for Further Reading). Now, I want to share some history with you and the reality of the present situation. There is good news and bad news.

The Bad News: One Hundred Years of Whole–Word Methods

Universal education began gathering momentum in the late nineteenth century and was responsible for launching a century of whole-word reading methods throughout the English-speaking world. A whole-word method is the antithesis of phonics, which teaches the alphabet principle—that our writing system is a code in which individual speech sounds (called *phonemes*) are assigned a letter symbol. Whole-word methods are based on the false belief that children can memorize letter sequences standing for whole words *by sight* (visual memory alone) with no understanding of what the individual letters represent. This makes learning to read exactly like memorizing the telephone directory—48673972 = football.

In part, whole-word methods were a reaction to the problems created by universal education, a cataclysmic event set into motion by the stroke of a pen. To meet the immediate demands set forth by legislators, teachers were hastily trained, schools were hastily built, and crammed with far too many children. Reports indicate that seventy to one hundred children per classroom was not uncommon. Colleges for teacher training were set up almost overnight, and the 'professors' in these new colleges knew little more about teaching reading than the students they taught. Into this vacuum stepped self-appointed 'education gurus,' people who made up for their lack of experience in the classroom with dogmatic opinions and political clout. In the opinion of this self-selected elite, phonics was a no-win solution requiring too much individual attention. Instead, it was argued, children should be taught with flash cards from the front of the room. This method became known as *look-say*, and programs of this type entered the schools in the 1920s. Flash cards were soon overtaken by *basal readers* ('basal' meaning basic and comprehensive). These were meaning-based whole-word methods with a heavy emphasis on vocabulary work targeted to the words for the day, usually common words the children already knew. Various basal programs were churned out by the newly fledged educational publishing houses, complete with detailed scripted lessons for the teacher and graded readers for the children.

Whole-word methods have a long shelf life, and basal readers will be well known to many parents, and certainly to grandparents. By the mid-1960s, a survey showed that 95 percent of American children were being taught to read with one of the basal programs. The lessons begin with the teacher introducing the words for the day and a discussion of each word's meaning. Next, children see each word in print and are asked to memorize them 'by sight.' These words are seen once more in a series of dull and repetitive books with characters like Janet and John, and Dick and Jane.

"Come, Jane, come. Come see me. See me play. Come and see. Come play, Jane," said Dick.

"See me, come and see. I can swing. See me swing. Come and swing, Jane," said Dick.

Words were introduced slowly over weeks and months, and reading vocabulary expanded at a meager 500 words per year. Creative writing and spelling were nowhere to be seen until second or third grade.

In the late 1960s, a third whole-word approach was proposed by American educator Kenneth Goodman, largely as a reaction against the narrowness and dullness of the basal reader programs. This method became known as 'whole language' and it caused a sensation around the English-speaking world. Teachers loved it and for quite understandable reasons: First, good children's literature was back in the classroom. Second, teachers were no longer directly responsible for teaching children to read, write, or spell. Their job was to read books at story time while children listened and followed along, and then to watch at a distance as children freely wrote about whatever they chose, teaching themselves to spell in the process. It didn't matter that what children wrote couldn't be deciphered by anyone, including the child who had just written it. *The actual teaching of the alphabet code was nowhere in sight.*

Whole language is rather like a religion, based on faith rather than fact. Goodman believes that learning to read is like learning a natural language, and it will occur spontaneously if children are exposed to books written in natural language, and not the stilted and artificial language of basal readers. Children will learn by osmosis when they 'read along' with the teacher in little books while she reads aloud from a big book. When children read alone, they are encouraged to use 'all their cueing systems'—guessing unknown words from context clues, grammar, the illustrations on the page, plus any knowledge of the alphabet they might have picked up along the way. As Goodman put it, "Reading is a psycholinguistic guessing game." Children learn to spell by inventing their own spelling system ("invented spelling") during creative writing.

Note the logical implications of this approach. If learning to read is as natural as learning to talk, then when a child fails to learn to read, it must be *his fault*. Perhaps he's developmentally delayed or has a perceptual problem or an 'attention-deficit disorder.' As no direct instruction is necessary, teachers are not responsible for failure. Children are simply passed up the system (advanced to the next grade level) with the assumption that they will ultimately teach themselves to read, write, and spell. Whole language promises everything but delivers nothing.

Goodman had no scientific support for his claims, and the whole-language movement is noticeably reluctant to conduct research. Meanwhile, it created an educational disaster. The definitive proof finally came with the first rigorous national tests in The National Assessment of Educational Progress (NAEP 1992, 1994) on 140,000 American nine-year-olds. California was of particular interest, because it was the largest state to mandate whole language. Imagine everyone's shock when California came in dead last in the nation with a functional illiteracy rate of nearly 60 percent. Kenneth Goodman was quoted as saying: "Whole language is dead." The situation wasn't much better in the other states. The average functional illiteracy rate for the nation was 43 percent, a figure that has remained unchanged since 1992 (despite state and local action). Functional illiteracy is a measure of the child's ability to identify and use relevant information in passages that gradually increase in length and difficulty. It is a global measure of both decoding and comprehension, the ability to read and understand grade-appropriate text.

The dismal test scores were a wake-up call for legislators who at last began to take notice of parents' complaints. California quickly reversed the mandate and spent millions of taxpayers' dollars on teacher retraining. News of the disaster spread around the English-speaking world. It was partly responsible for the British government implementing the National Literacy Strategy in 1998, which cost taxpayers £57 million ($94,000,000).

Prompt action does not guarantee good solutions, however, and it did not do so here. Parents, legislators, and reading researchers urged a return to phonics, but after a hundred years of neglect, no one was quite sure what phonics was. This suggestion was met by stiff opposition, not only from the teachers, but also from the educational establishment, including professors of education, curriculum specialists, and teachers' unions. And they had strong support behind the scenes from the educational publishing houses, the source of those very expensive, beautifully illustrated 'big books,' and the millions of little books that children used to read along, and the well-stocked classroom libraries.

The outcome was a compromise. Phonics advocates were right. Whole language advocates were right. New untried ideas, based on limited scientific evidence of dubious quality, were right. The reign of eclecticism had begun. In the United States, eclecticism, or the "balanced approach," means teaching a hodgepodge of different reading methods in a fixed progression. The underlying principle is based on the myth that young children *can't hear* the individual consonant and vowel sounds (phonemes) that are the basis for an alphabetic writing system.

Instead, children need extensive training in phonological awareness: learning to isolate or segment words from sentences, syllables from words, syllable fragments from syllables, and finally
phonemes from syllables and words. Children engage in games
and exercises like clapping out syllable beats (*camp-ing, un-
happ-y, tel-e-phone*) and finding the rhyming endings in 'word
families' like *at* in *cat, bat, hat*. Only after this training can children move on to practice segmenting and blending phonemes in
words (/d/ - /o/ - /g/ in *dog*).

There is no evidence to support this phonological progression as relevant to mastering the code, and a mountain of evidence against it. Research shows that even babies can hear
phonemes quite well, thank you very much, and by age three
children can easily blend isolated phonemes into a word, and
identify this word among a set of pictures: /d/-/o/-/g/ = dog.
Meanwhile, research shows that teaching children to isolate and
segment words, syllables, and word families is a complete waste
of time, while teaching the phoneme-letter correspondences *from
the outset* is the key to success.

No other document reveals the garbled logic of eclecticism
better than the National Literacy Strategy, a set of rigid guidelines laid down by the Department of Education in England. The
NLS mandates a 'literacy hour' for all primary schools in the
United Kingdom and specifies the exact elements to be taught for
a precise number of minutes. If a teacher followed this to the letter, it would take three years or more to teach the basic alphabet
code, because it is tangled up with a hodgepodge of other activities similar to those described above. As the literacy hour
unfolds, what children learn at 9:00 is contradicted by what they
are taught at 9:15, and this, in turn, is contradicted by what they
are taught at 9:25, and so forth. Thus, it comes as no surprise
that recent testing on the efficacy of the NLS shows that it too is

a dismal failure. Children scored no higher than they did with whole language on its own.

The bad news is a double whammy for parents and their children. Obviously, children are at high risk for reading failure in classrooms that promote either pure whole language or eclecticism. This puts the family in the hot seat, forcing parents to be proactive rather than reactive. Parents are virtually obligated to take on the job of teaching reading *before* their child gets to school *in case* there are problems later on.

The Good News

In the nineteenth century, the English educator and self-taught linguist Isaac Pitman (of shorthand fame) made a huge breakthrough toward designing an effective reading program for teaching the English writing system, one where *every child* learns to read in a short amount of time. Teaching children to read was simple, quick, and foolproof in many European countries, but not in England. The primary difference lay in the transparency of the code. In a transparent writing system, each sound unit is assigned one symbol, which is the case in Italy, Spain, Sweden, Finland, Norway, Germany, and Austria. In contrast, the English writing system is highly opaque, with multiple spellings for most sounds and multiple ways to decode letter symbols. Transparent refers to the fact that it is *obvious* how the code works. An obvious code easy to teach, and easy to learn. An opaque code, on the other hand, is difficult to teach (easy to teach badly), putting children at high risk for confusion and failure.

Pitman recognized that the solution was to level the playing field—to set up initial instruction *as if* the code were transparent. He created what I call an *artificial transparent alphabet*, assigning each of the forty English phonemes to a letter of the alphabet or special symbol. We'll look at the reasons why this helps later. Nellie Dale, a talented classroom teacher, adapted this approach for beginning readers and modified this to a Basic Code: forty phonemes and their most common spellings. The results were astonishing. It was possible to teach Dale's method from the front of the room to as many as seventy children, every one of whom learned to read. Despite the popularity of Dale's program on both sides of the Atlantic, it too fell victim to universal education.

The good news is that there is a new crop of reading programs with the same basic features as Dale's program, and these programs produce astonishing results on standardized reading tests, verifying Dale's claims. There are several to recommend for the classroom and for home use. What is especially significant about these programs is how much they resemble one another in basic principles. All, for example, employ a Basic Code as a beginning step. The truth is that we do know exactly what works and what does not. Teaching reading (and spelling) does not have to be a lottery. It is simple to teach a child to read when you know what you're doing.

There is more good news. Some teachers have become aware of these good programs, and have adopted them for their classrooms, despite objections from state and local officials. The highly successful classroom program *Jolly Phonics* can be found in scores of classrooms across Great Britain and Canada. Other good programs (*Lippincott*, *Best Practice Phonics*, *Phono-Graphix*) are used in many schools in the United States and the United Kingdom. You may get lucky. With a little detective work you can find out whether one of these programs, or one like them, is used in your local school. The following section provides details about these excellent programs along with important background information about how writing systems work.

A Parent's Guide to Reading Methods

Knowledge is power. Knowing exactly how and why certain methods of reading instruction are effective will give you a tremendous advantage and a boost in confidence. It will sustain you in your decision to teach your child to read. It will allow you to deal calmly with the school system, secure in your knowledge and convictions, while being able to evaluate what you are told by the school. Parents often have difficulty getting good information from the school or from a classroom teacher. For example, how is a parent supposed to evaluate statements like these?

- Susan is a little delayed developmentally. She'll catch up in due course.
- We don't teach writing at this age; children are too young. We use plastic letters in the second grade. I'm glad Nigel can write all his letters, but many children can't. Please have him do this at home for now.
- I make sure that all the children learn the twenty-six letter-names before they move on to invented spelling. This way the children have a firm foundation.
- Yes, we spend a lot of time on Big Books and group reading, because that is the only way children can learn to read in context and build vocabulary.
- We have a strong emphasis on sight word reading at this school, because, over time, all words are read by sight.
- I like to teach lots of rhyming patterns and rhyming games, because children need this listening practice before they learn how to use an alphabet.
- In this school, we tailor reading instruction to each child's learning style.

Each of these statements should be a red flag, and you need to know why. The main reason that reading instruction is in such a mess is that the reading programs throughout the twentieth century were set up with no understanding of how writing systems work or how children learn.

How a Writing System Works

A WRITING SYSTEM is a code that represents units of speech with written symbols. That is, speech sounds are *encoded* by a set of symbols, and these symbols can then be *decoded* to recover the sounds. This is like any other code: Morse code, musical notation, a number system, or computer languages. To set up a writing system from scratch, the first decision is to choose a speech unit as the basis for the code, because, as we have seen, there are several to choose from.

The history of writing systems provides critically important lessons about what does and does not work. For example, in the five-thousand-year history of writing systems, no system, living or dead, ever used the whole word as the unit (basis) for the system. This is rather remarkable considering the fact that the educational establishment has argued for one hundred years that English-speaking children should learn to read by memorizing whole words by sight. The archaeological record reveals a highly consistent pattern. Ancient scholars did indeed try to design a writing system in which symbols stood for whole words. But in every case, when they reached 2,000 word/symbol pairs or less, this idea was scrapped, and they switched to a unit of speech below the level of the word. The 2,000-word ceiling was so consistent over time, across continents, and from one culture to the next, that it constitutes a kind of law. It tells us about the limitations of human memory. Humans can't remember abstract visual patterns very well, much less remember which abstract pattern goes with which particular word.

Furthermore, the 2,000-word limit is an *ultimate limit*. It is *all* that people can memorize even with years of training. We know this from the Japanese, who retain a fair number of ancient word symbols (kanji) in their writing system. It takes Japanese children twelve years, from early primary school to the end of secondary school, to memorize the 1,860 kanji required for high school graduation. Of course, 2,000 words doesn't come close to the average size of spoken vocabulary. People need about 50,000 words just to carry on an ordinary conversation. There are 250,000 words in a good college dictionary. *The Oxford Companion to the English Language* estimates that there are around one million words in the English language. This is the reason why the main writing system in Japan is based on the consonant-vowel (CV) unit and not the whole word.

The human brain is a word sponge, and people effortlessly acquire enormous vocabularies that continue to increase throughout life. Human memory thrives on *meaning* and falters without it. This is why people have such difficulty memorizing abstract (meaningless) patterns. To get some sense of how difficult this is, imagine a sheet of paper covering the floor of a large room. On this paper are written 2,000 abstract symbols like <> (*) # &, set out in 40 rows of 50 symbols each. Think about what it would be like to memorize these 2,000 symbols *and then to* remember which one went with which word, and you will have some idea of why a whole-word writing system can't work.

We have had a century of whole-word methods in which children learn that random letter sequences stand for whole words. Imagine you're a child and know nothing about alphabet codes or writing systems. You are in the same room and looking at the same sheet of paper, but this time it's covered with 2,000 random letter sequences made up of the twenty-six letters of the alphabet. The sequences come in various lengths. Some are as short as one (*I, a*) and some are as long as eight or more (*wonderful, tomorrow, submarine, brontosaurus*). Imagine having to memorize these letter sequences by sight *as if there were no code* AND to remember which letter string went with which word in the language. This, in a nutshell, is why a whole-word writing system and a whole-word teaching method *can't work, never did work, and never will work.* This is what is wrong with the teaching methods in our schools.

There is another reason—a logistical reason—why a whole-word writing system can't work. Vocabulary is constantly changing. Old words drop out and new words are added daily. If every new word (or people's names) required a unique (random) letter string, when new words, such as *computer, software, hardware, digital, Web site, hacker, nerd*, enter the language, we would need a commission (a National Writing Board) working around the clock to set up new letter strings for each new word. These would have to be communicated in weekly mailings sent to all citizens to keep them up to date. In short, whole-word writing isn't a system. *It isn't a code: There is no way to spell (or read) words you have never seen before.*

It is for these reasons that every writing system in the five-thousand-year history of writing systems was designed for a speech unit *below the level of the word.* The first major advantage is that there are far fewer speech units than words, no matter which unit is chosen. This makes it possible to memorize them fairly quickly. More importantly, these speech units are fixed in number. New words are created all the time by recombining speech sounds that are 'legal' in our syllable structure: *storch, gump, infing, tronget* are legal—*bgoik, fweng, toobf* are not. The speech sounds themselves take centuries to alter, if they alter at all. The majority of phonemes in our language are the same as they were in the ninth century when King Alfred resurrected the English writing system after the Vikings destroyed all the libraries.

There are four types of speech units used in the writing systems of the world. Scholars select among these possibilities using this simple principle: Choose the largest unit (easiest to hear) that doesn't overload memory (small in number, hence most efficient to learn). There is the *syllable* for languages with very few syllable types, like Chinese, *consonant-vowel pairs* (CV diphones) for languages where the majority of words are built from sequences of these pairs, like the languages of India, Southeast Asia, Japan, and Korea (the English word: *potato* is an example of a CV-CV-CV word). *Consonants only* were chosen for languages where consonant sequences carry the meaning load and always stay in a fixed sequence, like Hebrew and Arabic (vowels are added by the reader). Last, but not least, individual *consonants and vowels* (phonemes) are used for languages with a complex syllable structure and no repetitive or systematic speech patterns (European languages).

Writing systems based on the phoneme are known as alphabets. Alphabets are extremely economic. Although English is a highly complex language with sixteen syllable types and over fifty-five thousand legal syllables in the language, *it has only forty phonemes*, making them extremely economic (easy) to learn. But phonemes are the smallest unit of sound that people can hear, and they can be hard to disentangle. An alphabetic writing system is a trade-off between using a sound unit that's easy to memorize but hard to hear. Phonemes overlap in speech and go by too fast for us to notice them. In fact, most adults aren't aware of phonemes or that they even exist, unless someone points them out. This is why it is critical for children learning to read an alphabetic writing system to be made aware of phonemes (and ONLY phonemes) and how they are ordered in words. These forty phonemes, and the letters that represent them, need to be taught.

Why Eclectic or Balanced Methods Don't Work

THERE'S ANOTHER RULE about writing systems: All successful writing systems past or present are based on *one unit of speech and never more than one.* If the syllable is adopted as the unit (China), syllable symbols are designed; if the consonant-vowel unit (CV) is chosen (India), CV symbols are designed, and if the phoneme is chosen, phoneme symbols (letters) are designed. This is obvious when you think about it. The golden rule for designing and teaching a writing system is: Never mix speech units. This would completely destroy the logic of the code. To teach a writing system properly means teaching only the particular speech unit that the writing system was designed for, how many of these units there are, and which symbol goes with which sound.

Think of the confusion created by the eclectic teaching methods described in the previous section. In effect, these methods teach four or more writing systems simultaneously. Children learn (haphazardly) that different-sized units of sound are represented by different-sized lengths of letter sequences. A whole word (sight word) is the entire letter string. A syllable is a smaller segment of this string; a word family is a segment of a syllable, and so forth. But even this isn't straightforward. Single letters (*a* and *i*) stand for whole words, syllables, and phonemes all at the same time. The four letters in the word *fast* stand for one word, one syllable, and four phonemes. The five letters in *table* stand for one word, two syllables, and five phonemes. The seven letters in *through* stand for one word, one syllable, and three phonemes. How could anyone learn to read if all these speech units mattered?

Eclectic methods force children to work out *on their own* how to scan or group letter sequences to represent these different units of sound. If children must constantly shift between *the size of the speech unit* and *the length of the letter string* as they read text, nothing is stable or constant. This makes it nearly impossible to learn to read, unless the child stumbles onto a better way. If children learn four or five ways to break up a word, how, for example, should they choose among these options to decode the word *plant*?

plant: whole word = random letter-string method
pl-ant: initial consonant blend (CC) + rhyme unit (the *ant* family) method
pl-a-nt: initial consonant blend (CC) + vowel + final consonant blend (CC) method
p-l-a-n-t: the alphabet method (correct)

This is a simple example in which each sound is represented by one letter. But English spelling is much more complicated than this. For one thing, we have only twenty-six letters for forty sounds in the language. This problem was solved by pairing letters to stand for one sound. These letter-pairs are known as *digraphs*. Most English words contain digraphs, as *sh* in *ship*, *oo* in *room*, *oa* in *boat*. Some spellings contain as many as four letters for one sound, such as *ough* in *through* and *igh* in *high*.

Understanding How Our Alphabet Works Helps Us Know How to Teach It

We have an alphabetic writing system, and we can't try to turn it into something else without derailing a large number of children. As we have seen from the NAEP reports, up to 60 percent in a whole-language classroom, 43 percent nationwide. A good reading method should teach our alphabetic writing system, nothing more nor less, and *every child* should be reading.

As noted above, some alphabetic writing systems are better than others. In a transparent alphabet, the code is consistent: the sound /p/ is always encoded (spelled) with the letter *p*, and the letter *p* is always decoded (read) with the sound /p/. With only modestly good instruction, the children can easily see that this is a code, and that the code is reversible (reading/spelling are two sides of one coin).

By contrast, in English, there are multiple ways to spell most sounds and multiple ways to decode most letter(s). The sound /ou/ can be spelled <u>ou, ow, ough</u> as in *out, cow, bough*. The spelling <u>ou</u> can be read /ou/, /ōo/, /aw/, /uh/, /oe/ as in *shout, soup, cough, touch, soul*. The spelling <u>ow</u> can be read /ou/, /oe/ as in *cow, tow*, and the spelling <u>ough</u> can be read /ou/, /oe/, /ōo/ as in *bough, dough, through*. The sound /ee/ has the most spellings (ten altogether), and all except <u>ee</u> can be decoded several different ways: <u>ea</u> (bead), for example, is decoded as /e/ in *head* and /ae/ in *great*.

Our spelling system has been a major bone of contention for over four hundred years. Until 1755, when Samuel Johnson standardized spelling in his famous dictionary, people could spell any way they felt like it, which made the teaching of reading and spelling almost impossible. But Johnson's dictionary standardized spelling for individual *words*; it did not standardize spelling for *sounds*. This problem never got solved. Nor can this be solved today, because changing the spelling system would be too disruptive and expensive. For example, it would be a simple matter to adopt the most common spelling <u>ee</u> for the sound /ee/ instead of the 10 spellings currently in use, but we would find this exceedingly odd: *seem, dreem, shee, scheem, beeleeve, reeceeve, luckee, kee, radeeo, mareen,* instead of: seem, dream, she, scheme, believe, receive, lucky, key, radio, marine.

The solution for how to structure lessons so that spelling is easy to teach is beyond the scope of this book. Readers are referred to my previous books for a thorough analysis of the higher level of the code (see Suggestions for Further Reading). Here, I will emphasize beginning reading. The question is, what is the best way to teach our formidable alphabet code so that children are never confused, and so that the advanced spelling level can be taught with no change in logic?

Most parents believe (while most teachers do not) that the best way to teach an alphabetic writing system is to train children to 'sound out' words using the alphabet principle. Methods that do this are called phonics. But there are literally hundreds of different phonics programs, some very good, some very bad. To help sort this out, phonics programs can be divided into two basic types: those that teach from the letter to the sound, and those that teach from the sound to the letter. This is an extremely important demarcation for the following reasons:

1. Programs that teach from the sound to the letter are set up with a Basic Code—the forty sounds in English and their most common spelling.
2. Programs of this type are easy to teach (transparent) and work for all children.
3. Programs of this type are few in number, so it's not hard to identify them.

Based on this demarcation, I will briefly describe 'letter-driven' phonics programs, such as those that teach the 'twenty-six sounds of the twenty-six letters'—a method that leaves seventeen English phonemes unidentified. Then I will focus on those programs that teach the alphabet principle correctly, and present the features of these successful programs in more detail.

The Origin of Letter-Driven Phonics

THE FIRST FULL-FLEDGED phonics program of any type was written by Noah Webster in 1783, and became known as the blue-backed speller or the American speller. Webster's speller became the top selling reading/spelling program on both sides of the Atlantic for nearly one hundred years. Webster was gifted in languages and was well aware that phonemes (consonants and vowels) are the basis for an alphabet code. In the introduction to the first edition of the speller, he set out thirty-eight phonemes in English, and the different ways each sound could be spelled. (Later, this information was relegated to an appendix.) Although he used this information to set up the lessons, the logic was backward.

The actual lessons were letter-driven and provided no knowledge or insight about sounds in speech, how many there were, or why or when the same sounds had multiple spellings. Multiple spellings were included, but not in any way to draw attention to them. The lessons consisted of memorizing columns of printed words. The only organizing principles were that (1) words increased in syllable length as the lessons progressed, and (2) where possible, word lists were set up in rhyming families in alphabetical order: *ban, can, Dan, fan, man, pan, ran, tan, van.* These vowel-consonant units have nothing to do with the alphabet code (*an* is not a phoneme), so setting up words this way is more misleading than helpful. Furthermore, most English words don't fit into rhyming word families in the first place.

Webster's speller introduced the logic of the code backwards from letter to sound: The letter *b makes* the sound /b/. The correct logic is from sound to print, the direction the code was written: The sound /b/ is written *b*. Letters are assigned to sounds. Sounds are not assigned to letters. Nor do letters *have* sounds or *make* sounds. *People make sounds.*

This may seem like splitting hairs, but it matters a great deal when you have to teach an opaque writing system. Children are magical thinkers. They don't find it the least bit odd to be told that 'letters make sounds' ("This letter makes the sound /p/"). If you encourage children to think magically, they will most certainly oblige you, as we have seen throughout this book. But this magical system starts to fall apart at the point where the teacher tells the children that a letter 'says' more than one sound. Here's an example:

> Last week we learned that the letter O says /ah/, like in
> the word *hot.*
> Today we're going to learn that the letter O says /oe/,
> like in the word *told.*
> Later we'll learn that the letter O says /oo/ like in the
> word *to.*

Clearly, these magic talking letters can't be trusted. At this point, some children who thought they were 'getting it' will become convinced they did not and may give up entirely. (There are over three hundred ways to decode letters and digraphs in English. But there aren't three hundred sounds in the English language, so starting off with this logic gets you into trouble in a hurry.)

Linguistic Phonics

THE SECOND TYPE of phonics program first appeared at the end of the nineteenth century with the application of linguistics to reading instruction, as noted above. Nellie Dale's program was based on the forty sounds (phonemes) of the language, *not on the letters of the alphabet.* The main innovation was the Basic Code, with each sound mapped to its most common spelling. A Basic Code allows the teacher and the children to experience an alphabet that was properly designed. Children can see the structure of an alphabetic writing system directly, that letters (symbols) are assigned to the sounds in *their* speech, that there is a fixed number of these sounds (forty) that never change. A Basic Code reveals the logic of a writing system, the fact that it's a code, and that codes are both *predictable* and *reversible.* The sound /b/ is *encoded* b, and the letter b can be *decoded* back to /b/. This knowledge makes a tremendous difference to children's confidence and to their reading skill. (The Basic Code is set out at the end of this chapter.)

The Basic Code temporarily shelves the problem of how to teach multiple spellings for the same sound, while, at the same time providing a platform or an access point to the rest of the spelling system. (Teaching the code backwards from letter to sound does not do this.) It also provides the best spelling option when children don't know how to spell a word: *When in doubt, spell it in Basic Code.* This means that from the beginning, children can write words and stories that they and other people can read *phonetically*, even if the spelling looks a little odd.

A second important spin-off from this approach is that with a consistent logic in place, our awkward spelling system becomes much easier to teach. The child knows that our language has a fixed number of sounds that never change (an end point), and that these sounds are coded into letters or digraphs. This makes it possible for the teacher to say:

We learned the main way to spell the sound /oe/, like in the word home, but there's another way to spell it. It's

spelled with the letter o in words like ***told*** and ***most***.
Today, we're going to look at these kinds of words.

Contrast this with the teacher who told the children the letter O says /ah/ in *hot* and /oe/ in *told*, and /oo/ in *to*. From a child's perspective, if letters can keep making more and more sounds, and the number of sounds these letter can make appears to go on to infinity, how could you ever learn to read?

Because few educators understand the logic of a writing system, the nature of an alphabet code, or how our spelling system works, it is not surprising that professors of education and the teachers they train have no idea how to teach reading *or* spelling. This is why we have whole-word methods or balanced methods. This is why spelling instruction consists of lists of words chosen at random by the teacher or by the authors of classroom spelling programs. It explains why reading and spelling instruction are taught in different lessons, on different days. Because reading and spelling are rarely connected, it's common for children to be given spelling words they *can't read*. I have worked with children who can memorize the weekly spelling words by sight and score 100 percent on every spelling test week after week, only to forget how to spell these words a day or two later. They have no logic for managing the code because they were never taught it. Most don't even know there *is* a code, because their teachers don't know this either. It's quite common for very poor readers with high verbal memory skills to get an A on every spelling test, yet their teachers don't find this odd!

Dale introduced a number of other innovations. Here are the major features of a lesson sequence. As Dale taught these lessons to seventy children from the front of the room, we know that classroom size is no particular handicap to teaching children to read, and that successful methods can work from the front of the room. (Less than ideal conditions are no excuse for ineffective reading instruction.)

1. Lessons began with a sentence or short story featuring one of the forty phonemes to be taught. *Letter names were never used* and were actively discouraged.

2. Children were asked to find a secret word in the story and listen to the first sound of that word: /p/ as in *pig*.

3. Attention was directed to the physical act of how the sound is produced—the parts of the mouth that were working to make the sound. Children checked if the sound was voiced (vocal cords vibrating) or unvoiced, by touching their windpipe. (Try it: /b/ is made by compressing the lips and popping them open, and is *voiced*—cords vibrating; /p/ is made the same way, but is *unvoiced*.)

4. After a few sounds were taught and practiced, children were shown large wooden letters that represented those sounds. Dale designed a frame to hold the letters, which stood at the front of the room. Categories of speech sounds were grouped together on the frame.

5. After each letter was introduced and hung on the frame, children copied the letter many times on a blackboard inside the lids of their desks, saying the *sound* (*not the letter name*) as they wrote it.

6. After several sounds were introduced, children learned to identify first, last, and middle sounds in three-sound words, and to blend sounds into words: /c/-/u/-/p/—*cup*.

7. The letters for each word were assembled on the

frame at the front of the room, and copied by the children on their blackboards. Children were encouraged to discover new words spelled with the same sounds: *cup, up, pup*.

8. As the lessons progressed, common spelling alternatives were introduced.

She engaged the children in various activities and movement. Children pretended they were a letter or a sound and stood in a row to represent a word. One at a time, each child made his sound, or held up his letter, and the class blended the sounds into the word. Children were asked to work on the wooden frame directly to change letters to make new words.

Sadly, Dale's program faded away and died, but her ideas did not, and programs were developed that were similar in structure and logic. These programs are important, because for the first time, there is solid research support for their effectiveness.

In the mid-1960s, there was a vast experiment in the United States to determine, once and for all, which reading method was best. The study involved nine thousand first graders in hundreds of classrooms across America. The teachers in these classrooms were trained to teach a particular method. Various phonics or linguistic-type methods were compared to the basal method adopted by the schools. Half the classes in each school were taught the traditional basal program, and the other half with some type of phonics approach.

The method most similar to Dale's was an American program designed by Glenn McCracken and Charles Walcutt, called *Basic Reading*, and published by Lippincott. It started with the Basic Code organized around the forty English phonemes, and taught from sound to print. Equal time was devoted to practice in reading, spelling, and writing, and all three skills were connected in the lessons. This program led to a rapidly increasing reading vocabulary. By the end of first grade, children had learned to decode over two thousand words, ten times as many words as in the basal reader classrooms. And because these children were being taught to *decode*, whereas children in basal reader classrooms were not, they could read lots of words they'd never been taught. Twenty-two percent of the lesson time was devoted to writing, compared to zero for children in the basal reader classrooms. Children copied words and took spelling dictation, neither of which were done in the basal classrooms.

At the end of the school year, children were given nine standardized tests normed on large numbers of children. The tests measured accuracy in decoding real words and nonsense words (*storp*, *kag*), spelling, reading comprehension, reading fluency, and basic phonics skills, such as knowledge of letter-sound correspondences. The five hundred children in the Lippincott classrooms were consistently superior on every test to every other comparison group. They scored six months ahead of the children taught by other methods and six months above national norms.

Unfortunately, due to a major error in data handling and statistics, the results from this study were reported incorrectly, leading to the conclusion that no method was consistently superior from one classroom to the next. The true results, described above, were revealed when the data were reassessed.*

Tragically, this monumental study had virtually no impact on

---

*For readers knowledgeable about statistics, student scores were combined within classrooms, drastically reducing the statistical power of the study. This had the effect of shifting the focus of the study from one comparing *children* learning specific methods to one comparing *classrooms* (teachers perhaps?). Technically, this means that the "within subjects variance" is coming from the classrooms, and not from the *children* within classrooms.

promoting good reading methods, misleading people for decades into believing that all methods were equally valid, and that methods didn't matter! The Lippincott program (originally called Basic Reading and now known as Lippincott, after the publisher) disappeared off the radar screen and is not in common use today. However, in a recent report by the National Reading Panel, surveying research on reading programs over the past twenty years, the Lippincott program continued to shine in comparisons with other methods.

Today there are several new reading programs that have had even greater success. All were developed by classroom teachers, or by people who work with poor readers in a clinic. *Jolly Phonics* (United Kingdom) was created by Sue Lloyd for four- and five-year-olds in the classroom and can be used at home. *Best Practice Phonics* (United Kingdom) was created by Ruth Miskin for four-to-six-year-olds in the classroom, with a special focus on teaching non-English-speaking children. *Phono-Graphix* (United States) was created by Carmen and Geoffrey McGuinness. It was designed originally for children with reading problems, and then was adapted for home and classroom use. *Jolly Phonics* has received the most attention from researchers. Other United States programs like *DISTAR* and *Open Court Reading* are similar in nature and have produced good results in well-conducted studies, though not as consistently. Classroom programs are reviewed in depth in my book *Early Reading Instruction* (see Suggestions for Further Reading).

The most successful programs share similar features: a Basic Code, an emphasis on the sounds of the language (forty phonemes), sound-to-letter orientation, and lessons that move to meaning as soon as possible: sounds to letters to *words*. Children learn to listen to and *write* phonemes in all positions in a word: initial, middle, final, and to segment and blend sounds into the words. Lessons begin with simple words and words gradually become more complex. (This is opposite to whole language, whose proponents argue that word length makes no difference in how well you remember the word.) Lessons move ahead rapidly, and children are reading simple books after eleven or twelve weeks.

Handwriting is another emphasis. In Lippincott and *Phono-Graphix*, children copy words they are learning to read, saying the sound as they write each letter, something Dale (and also Montessori) strongly recommended. *Jolly Phonics* has special handwriting activities, plus materials for tracing and copying letters and words. Children are taught how to hold a pencil and encouraged to write from the outset. *Best Practice Phonics* employs a sequence where children hear a sound spoken in isolation and write the letter. Next, they hear a word that starts with the same sound, and write the letter. Finally, they see an object whose name starts with the same sound, and write the letter. Later, children get individual whiteboards for spelling dictation. After they have written a word, they turn their boards to face the teacher. The teacher corrects errors and can use them as a lesson to clear up any misunderstandings.

There are several innovations in these new programs. The most important is the emphasis on speed (Dale's method took eighty-three lessons to reach the vowel digraphs.). When *Phono-Graphix* is used for one-on-one tutoring in the clinic, poor readers learn to read at their age level in twelve hours or less of clinical time, plus nightly parent support. This regimen works for all children regardless of their reading difficulty, age, or IQ. The initial findings on the first eighty-seven clients were published, and there is now a database on hundreds of children confirming these results. So far, there has been little valid research on the classroom version of this program.

Sue Lloyd (*Jolly Phonics*) did pioneering work on the optimum pacing for young children taught in the classroom. These lessons are taught to the whole class at the same time. She discovered that children do best with intensive instruction, and forget what they're taught when lessons are too brief or spread too far apart. Lloyd discovered by trial and error what has been documented in recent research, that children can't be 'eased' into learning to read by sporadic and nonsystematic lessons. But with systematic, intensive instruction, children from four and a half on can be taught to read and spell in about eleven weeks. This takes one hour per day of whole class lessons, thirty to forty minutes of individual reading/writing activities and games, plus parent support after school. The total time spent directly teaching reading is about sixty-five hours over this period.

Results from studies in England, Scotland, and Canada show that when *Jolly Phonics* is taught according to Lloyd's accelerated timetable, children make more than twice the gains on reading and spelling tests than when the program is taught more slowly or sporadically. When *Jolly Phonics* is taught as recommended, children average one year above age norms at the end of the school year on reading and spelling tests. These gains are maintained for at least five years, the longest time these children have been followed.

Jolly Phonics is equally effective for non-English-speaking children. In a study on immigrant children in London's impoverished docklands area, most of whom had little or no spoken English, reading accuracy and spelling were a year above national norms immediately after twelve weeks training and at follow-up one year later. This occurred even though the children's spoken vocabulary still lagged far behind.

Best Practice Phonics has not been tested in controlled studies, but independent testing was carried out on immigrant children in a London school who had just completed the program (age six and a half). Despite the fact that most of these children had little or no spoken English at the start of school, they scored a year or more above the national average on reading and spelling tests. Even though, like the docklands study, they also lagged behind in vocabulary.

These studies provide more evidence of the dissociation between vocabulary and reading mechanics mentioned in the introduction to this book. The non-English-speaking children continue to be delayed in their knowledge of the English language, while this didn't impair their ability to learn the English alphabet code. These results show that with appropriate methods, it is far easier to teach decoding than it is to increase children's oral language skills.

One way to discover which elements of a program matter is to compare common features of the successful programs, as I have done here. But there's another more powerful and convincing way to do this. It involves hours of sitting in classrooms recording what children actually do minute by minute. The goal in this type of study is to find out what is being taught during reading and language arts lessons, and to compare the amount of time spent on specific activities to progress in learning to read—*regardless of the method*. Three large-scale studies in the United States and Canada have been carried out using this approach, and the results are identical. The researchers compared the *time on task* (the number of minutes children were engaged in specific activities) to *test scores on decoding and reading comprehension* at the end of the school year, using correlational statistics. Only a few activities were strongly and positively correlated to the reading test scores. These were:

- Learning to identify phonemes plus practicing matching each phoneme to its common spelling
- Practicing analyzing phoneme sequences in words (segmenting, blending, phoneme identification) *using print*
- Tracing and copying letters, and writing *correctly spelled* words and phrases

These activities are all featured in the successful phonics methods described above. The big surprise was the large number of activities that had either no effect or a negative effect. Time spent on the following activities had no impact on reading skills (correlations between time spent on these tasks to subsequent reading test scores were close to zero):

- Learning letter names (any type of activity)
- Using letter names to read or spell words (*cow* is spelled "see oh double-you")
- Practicing on sound units larger than the phoneme, such as syllable segmenting, learning word families, or playing rhyming games
- Analyzing phoneme sequences in the absence of print (orally only)
- Reading along with the teacher or pretend reading
- Learning 'concepts of print'—such as how to turn pages, the left-to-right direction of our writing system, and punctuation

The following lessons were strong negative predictors (with correlations as high as −.70 and −.80). This means the *more* time spent on these activities, the *worse* the reading and spelling scores were:

- Memorizing whole words by sight
- Lessons on grammar and vocabulary

This is damning evidence against the typical early-reading activities taught in English-speaking countries. And it shows that memorizing whole words by sight is strongly detrimental to learning to read, while spending a lot of time teaching grammar and vocabulary slows progress in learning to read. This doesn't mean that learning grammar and vocabulary is 'bad for you'; it simply reflects a trade-off. It's much easier to learn to read if you focus your efforts on tasks that help you master the code. Thus, it's a better strategy for teachers to teach more complex language skills *after children master the code*, rather than while they are learning it.

These results also show that linguistic phonics programs, like those described above, have identified the most critical elements of good reading instruction. The tasks most likely to increase reading and spelling competence are e*xactly the same tasks* emphasized by the most successful reading programs. This is exciting news. It means we have the right answers, and that parents and teachers can be confident that they can teach reading successfully if they use any program that shares these features.

The facts are undeniable. If you want to teach children the alphabet code, *you need to teach the alphabet code!* Don't waste time teaching something that has nothing to do with the code. The more intensive the lessons, the sooner children can master the code, the sooner they can get on with reading interesting books, learn new vocabulary from their reading, do creative writing, and master the advanced spelling level.

This means that if parents intend to teach their four- or five-year-olds to read, they can't do this in a hit-or-miss fashion. Teaching reading needs careful planning. It's best to spend about thirty to forty minutes every other day (or every day) on the lessons. How fast parents can move ahead will depend on the child's willingness to participate, and this is related to the design features and age appropriateness of the lessons. I highly recommend that parents of young children use programs designed for this age group, and not try to modify programs designed for older children or for children with reading difficulties. Programs most suitable for home instruction are described at the end of the book.

There is a new program on the list, *Sound Steps to Reading*, which I designed specifically for home use for young children in the age range four to six years. It is based on the principles described above and contains all the materials a parent will need. There are forty 'parent stories,' which introduce each phoneme in the language, phoneme listening exercises for each sound, handwriting instruction and special exercises for linking up sounds and letters, word decoding exercises, spelling practice, and children's readers. *Sound Steps to Reading* incorporates most of the advanced spelling level for common English words. This will equate to a spelling level of a normal eight- or nine-year-old after about sixty to seventy hours of instruction (approximately one school year).

Teaching Your Child to Read

While some parents are eager to teach their child to read and are already trying to do so, most parents would be much happier if their child was taught at school. The problem is that there is no guarantee this will happen. Before you decide what to do, visit your local school and find out how they teach reading. You may be lucky. Be sure to read this chapter again before you go. It's possible that teachers may be using one of the programs listed above or a program similar to them. Talk to the teachers who teach beginning reading. A teacher who uses a good program will be having great success, and she'll be happy to tell you about it. Beware if a teacher doesn't brighten up when you mention reading; she will not be having much success. Talk to the school principal about his or her views on reading. Find out the latest test scores for the school and any plans for the future. If there is a good reading program in place, and you are impressed with the teacher, the children's enthusiasm, and their test scores, breathe a sigh of relief. (I guarantee this will happen for *some* of you, though not many.)

If you aren't pleased with what you find, you need to make a decision about whether or not to teach your child yourself. Unfortunately, there isn't much option between the school and you, or a substitute for you, such as a relative or friend. Reading clinics for poor readers aren't set up to teach beginning readers, and remedial reading methods don't include what beginners need, like training in handwriting, nor are most remedial programs particularly effective.

If you take on the task of teaching your child to read, there are a number of issues you need to keep in mind as you proceed through the lessons. The successful programs described above have some very important features in common. Three levels of understanding are integrated in every lesson: (a) speech is made up of individual sounds (phonemes); (b) we can represent these sounds by letters; (c) sequences of these letters stand for sounds in words.

The typical letter-first phonics methods and the phonics activity books found in bookstores usually don't teach these skills (or they teach them backwards) and should be avoided. It goes without saying that 'reading readiness' activities that have no effect (chanting letter names), or a detrimental effect (memorizing sight words), must be avoided.

Be aware that children don't make connections between abstract tasks taught at different times. The observational studies showed that teaching children to segment and blend sounds in words *without letters* had absolutely no effect on reading or spelling skill. Yet teaching the same skills in combination with letters had a huge effect. These connections have to be *taught* and need to be taught from the outset, otherwise you're wasting time.

The same conclusion was reached by the National Reading Panel, who recently reviewed thousands of studies on reading instruction and phoneme-awareness training. The panel reported that when lessons on phoneme analysis are *combined* with learning to match phonemes to letters, the impact on reading and spelling test scores more than doubles. This same principle applies to meaning. Children find it more difficult to learn individual phonemes and abstract letter shapes in isolation than when they're connected to *words* (meaning). Children should exercise these skills in the context of real language. For example, the first three lessons of *Sound Steps to Reading* are on the sound-to-letter connections for /p/, /o/, and /t/. At the end of the third lesson (day 3), the child can read and write four words: *pot, top, pop, tot*. As the lessons proceed, and more sounds are added, more and more words can be read and spelled. By the end of the sixth lesson (approximately 3 to 4 hours), the child can read and write little phrases like: *an ant on a pot* and *a tan man on a mat*.

Finally, the evidence is overwhelming that *sounds* + *letters* + *meaning* + *writing* need to be taught in the same lesson.

These facts have practical implications. It means there's no such thing as prereading exercises, no way to ease your child into learning to read, unless you want to take several years over it. If you intend to teach your child to read, you need to make a commitment: I will start teaching John to read on Saturday morning. Then schedule your week so that you and John get as much time as possible every day, or every other day, preferably no less than thirty minutes.

The following two lists summarize (a) the important information about the quirks of our alphabet writing system, and (b) the skills a child needs to acquire for maximum learning speed. The first list contains facts you should keep in mind while working with your child.

Important Facts for Parents to Keep in Mind

1. There are forty individual sounds (phonemes) in the English language. These sounds are the basis for our alphabet code, that is, what the code was written for.

2. There are twenty-six letters for the forty sounds. Three of these letters are wasted (could have been used for other sounds). These are *c*, which can represent /k/ or /s/ (*cat, cent*); *q(u)*, which represents the sound sequence /k/-/w/ (*quit*); and *x*, which represents the sound sequence /k/-/s/ (*exit*) or /g/-/z/ (*exist*).

3. The missing letter problem was solved by creating letter-pairs that work together to stand for one sound, such as *ch* (*church*) and *sh* (*ship*). These are called digraphs.

4. A few common words need to be taught by sight, because spellings are highly irregular. Examples are: *a, the, was, of, says* (uh, thuh, wuz, ov, sez). Don't teach sight words otherwise.

5. The Basic Code provided at the end of this chapter lists each sound and its most probable spelling (the spelling used in the largest number of words).

6. In English, most sounds can appear in all positions in a word: *bag/gab*; *top/pot*. This is known as transitivity, something young children *do not* understand. Many believe that the /b/ in *big* is a different sound from the /b/ in *cab*. Also, children find it easier to hear first sounds in words than middle and last sounds. Because of this, transitivity has to be taught:

"Listen. This is the same sound coming at the end of the word. Watch my mouth. I make this sound the same way if it comes at the beginning, in the middle, or at the end—*big, rabbit, cab).*"

7. DON'T USE LETTER NAMES WHEN TEACHING YOUR CHILD TO READ. Letter names have nothing to do with being able to read or spell. Letter names are a source of 'noise' and can cause confusion and learning delays. Letter names (alphabetical order) are important later, when children learn to use a dictionary.

Skills Your Child Needs to Learn

BE AWARE that this is not a sequence of instruction.

1. Be able to hear the forty individual sounds (phonemes) in words (/d/-/o/-/g/), and identify each sound in beginning, middle, and ending positions in words.
2. Be able to copy each of the twenty-six letter shapes and write them from memory.

3. Remember which sound goes with which letter(s).
4. Understand that two letters can stand for one sound: *sh* in *ship*.
5. Be able to blend three or more sounds into a word: /d/-/o/-/g/ is *dog*.
6. Be able to segment words (spoken or written) into sounds: *trip* is /t/-/r/-/i/-/p/.
7. Be able to say the sound the letter represents while writing it.
8. Read words containing sounds/letters that have been taught.
9. *Spell words from dictation containing the sounds/ letters that have been taught.*

Remember, the more these nine skills are combined in a lesson, the better.

Children need to trace, copy, and write sounds and words from memory (spelled correctly) as often as possible. (Don't use letter tiles, paper letters, or a computer keyboard.) Writing helps in many ways. First, the *physical act* of forming the letters forces the child to look closely at the features that make one letter different from another. The curve at the top of the letter *f* is missing from the letter *t*. Second, writing letters (left to right) trains the ability to *read* left to right. Third, saying each sound as the letter is written helps anchor the sound-to-letter connection in memory. This improves reading and spelling accuracy, and leads to greater ease (fluency) in written compositions. (Over time, this is done silently and not out loud.) Tracing patterns and letters or joining the dots to make pictures are among the few reading readiness activities that are valuable. Use a short pencil and model a good hand posture.

The Dyslexia Fallacy

Finally, I want to stress the important point that I hope this chapter has made clear, and this is the fact that problems with decoding and spelling are caused by something external to the child—poor methods of reading instruction compounded by poor instruction of our difficult spelling code. Reading problems *are not a property* of the child. It is common in the United States (though not in the United Kingdom) for the term 'dyslexia' (which is Greek for 'poor reading') to be used in a medical sense, as indicative of some kind of inherent disease or brain disorder. But cross-cultural studies show that if there was such a condition as dyslexia (a property of the child), children would be affected everywhere to the same extent, and certainly in countries with an alphabetic writing system. Yet poor readers (children who can't decode) are rare to nonexistent in many European countries.

When Heinz Wimmer asked sixty elementary school teachers in Salzburg, Austria, to refer their worst readers for additional testing, they referred 120 children out of approximately 1,500 children. These 'poor readers' astonished everyone by scoring 100 percent correct on a difficult reading (decoding) test, and doing nearly as well in spelling. Their only problem was that they read *too slowly*. The description of the teaching method employed in the Salzburg schools showed that it is nearly identical to the good methods described in this chapter. Another bonus for the Salzburg children is that the German alphabet code is transparent—there is generally one spelling for each sound.

As there are tried and true techniques for increasing reading fluency (speeding up the slow reader), the important message is that there is no dyslexia in Salzburg—and if there is no dyslexia in Salzburg, there can't be dyslexia anywhere else. If there was such a thing as *dyslexia*, caused by a brain anomaly due to faulty genes, the incidence of this disorder would be identical in every country that uses the same type of writing system. The only *biological* explanation that could account for the fact that there are no dyslexics in Salzburg (or Sweden, Finland, Italy, Spain, and many other countries), versus the millions of so-called dyslexics in English-speaking countries, would be that the English brain has evolved to learn (or not learn) the English alphabet code. As this is clearly nonsense, the obvious conclusion is that the biological explanation is false. And if the biological explanation is false, the environmental explanation must be true. There is no other alternative. For readers who are still unconvinced by this argument, it is spelled out in much more detail in my book *Why Our Children Can't Read*.

This is not to say that there aren't other factors that influence reading skill. By and large, these are the factors that have been addressed in this book—the importance of parents' input in promoting expertise in all areas of general language development like vocabulary growth and knowledge of syntax and semantics. However, these language abilities impact tests of reading *comprehension*, not tests of decoding and spelling. Even severely mentally retarded children can learn to decode, as Giuseppe Cossu's study on Down's syndrome children showed. The children in the London studies who had no spoken English, all learned to decode the English alphabet when taught properly.

The importance of general language skills to reading and academic success was highlighted in a study by Joseph Beitchman and his colleagues in Toronto. They tested 1,650 five-year-olds individually on various language tests prior to admission to school, then followed the children with language delays (plus a matched control group) until they were nineteen years old. The children identified with speech-motor problems *only* (about 6 percent of the children) were academically indistinguishable from the normal control children. However, the children with delays in general language, such as low vocabulary scores or poor grasp of syntax and semantics (about 12 percent of the total children) had far more difficulty academically. Only 25 percent recovered to normal levels. For the remainder, their language scores remained depressed, while reading and academic test scores declined to very low levels over time. By age nineteen, this group's vocabulary scores were below 80 on a standardized test (100 is normal). So far, we have no evidence on how much these serious language problems are due to heredity or to home environment, or are exacerbated by the school system, or all three. And while we know how important an enriched language environment is for good language development, we don't know how much it can compensate in extreme cases.

How Children Cope with Ineffective Reading Methods

If you have older children and one or more of them has a reading problem, you may be interested in knowing what strategy your child has adopted to compensate for his or her poor reading instruction. You will undoubtedly recognize your poor reader here.

Whole-Word Guessing

FOR ONE HUNDRED YEARS, English-speaking children have been taught by whole-word methods and asked to memorize words by sight. Some children survive this kind of instruction by figuring out a better way, but far too many fail. As learning to read by memorizing whole words is impossible, what do children do when they are taught with this method?

When we have a conversation, we're only aware of a 'transfer of meaning,' and pay little attention to individual sounds in speech. Children focus on meaning too, and this makes a whole-word reading method very appealing to a child. They believe that letter sequences stand for meaning directly. A whole-word strategy has some initial success because memorizing short words goes pretty well up to a point. It is precisely because whole-word methods link directly to meaning, and because initial learning goes quickly, that teachers like them.

But the honeymoon can't last. A child who memorizes letter strings as if they are telephone numbers will quit reading altogether by the end of the first grade. However, some children with a good vocabulary and good visual memory discover a trick, and work out a decoding strategy that holds up for a year or two longer before it begins to implode. By this time, the strategy will have hardened into a habit that can be difficult to break. Early success in reading followed by sudden and inexplicable failure, is the inescapable outcome for these children. This is devastating for the child and for his family, especially as a child's decoding strategy is invisible to parents and teachers, so no one understands what is happening. Children who stick with a whole-word strategy are at the greatest risk for reading failure and for being diagnosed with a 'learning disability' or 'dyslexia.'

Whole-word guessers are easy to spot if you know what you're looking for. There are two main types:

1. *Pure sight-word reader.* These children haven't figured out any way to decode print other than by pure visual

memorization. When their memory starts to fail, they revert to wild guesses (for example, they could read *box* as *fun*) and will soon stop reading altogether.

2. *Partial whole-word reader.* These children have figured out how to decode the first letter *phonetically.* Not knowing how to access the rest of the word, they focus on its length and shape (the global visual pattern of letter sequences) and try to match this *visually* with another word that looks like the printed word. (Think about how complicated this is.) When they misread a word, it is almost always another real word starting with the same sound. Here are typical errors taken from my study on reading strategies in a large group of normal children: *some* read as *soon, away* read as *alley, time* read as *then, family* read as *funny, wonderful* read as *waterfall, should* read as *shelled, money* read as *many, dangerous* read as *dinosaur.*

The children in this study were taught with a whole-language approach, plus some minimal phonics in kindergarten. Early in first grade nearly all the children were using a whole-word (sight-word) strategy. By the end of the first grade, the pure whole-word reader was guessing wildly or refusing to read altogether. One-third of the children had become partial whole-word readers. When these children were followed up in third grade, they *were still making the same proportion* of whole-word errors they made two years earlier, and were far and away the worst readers in the class. They had hit a memory ceiling and got stuck. Paradoxically, many of these children scored high on tests of vocabulary and visual memory, one reason they could scrape by with this strategy for so long.

Parents should know that a good remedial reading program can break a whole-word strategy quickly and get the child caught up in about twelve hours of one-on-one help. A poor remedial program may never break it. If 'dyslexia' was a property of the child due to some brain anomaly or disorder, as many people claim, where does the 'dyslexia' go in twelve hours of effective intervention?

Part-Word Assemblers

CHILDREN TAUGHT WITH an eclectic approach will also have reading problems. In fact, *both* whole-word and eclectic methods can lead to another decoding strategy that is typical of the *majority* of children. (It's also typical of many college students.) I call these children part-word assemblers. Part-word assemblers focus on familiar little words and word fragments *inside* words: *be, and, ing, mea, ind, hot, can.* Instead of decoding phoneme by phoneme from left to right, they scan back and forth across each word searching for familiar segments. Then they combine them into something like a word, not necessarily in the right order. Individual letters can be reused. When they misread a word (which is often) it is usually a nonsense word: *van-can-ant* for *vacant*. At this point, they search their memory for the closest sounding real word. Sometimes they find a match: *Oh, it's vacant!* More often they do not. Here are some typical errors from my study: *house* read as *hossoo, new* as *nee-wah, everyone* as *eve-lone, wonderful* as *won-fall, hotel* as *hot-let*. The children were well aware that these words made no sense. If you ask them what they're doing, they'll explain their strategy to you. It's quite intentional and conscious.

Parents who have older children with reading problems should determine their child's strategy. Ask your child to read aloud to you from something suitable for his age. He or she will fit one of these patterns. Remember: If your child has a reading problem, *it's not his fault*, and there's nothing wrong with his brain. The problem is ineffective and misleading reading instruction. Parents whose children aren't progressing in reading may also want to take on the task of teaching their child. The *Phono-Graphix* program is particularly suitable for older, poor readers, and is provided in a book for parents called *Reading Reflex*.

Summary

Growing a reader is a difficult and long-term task, one that involves parents' input every step of the way. Early interaction with your child impacts the general language skills that matter most for reading comprehension, and that turn out to be so important as the child advances through the school system. Reading comprehension is most highly correlated to *listening comprehension*, the ability to understand what people are saying. These two comprehension skills matter most for academic success from about the age of twelve on. Prior to this, schoolwork makes less of a demand on a child's vocabulary and general language skills.

On the other hand, learning to encode (spell) and decode (read) are simple skills, and if they are taught appropriately, any child can learn them. The problem comes when instruction is misleading, as it is most of the time in English-speaking countries. Unfortunately, until good reading programs like those described in this chapter are common in the classroom, parents are in the hot seat and almost obligated to take on this task themselves. I hope I have given you sufficient courage to attempt it. See Classroom Programs at the back of the book for descriptions of suitable programs. I wish you good luck in growing your reader!

THE BASIC CODE

CONSONANTS

SOUND	AS IN	SPELLING
/b/	big	b
/d/	dog	d
/f/	fun	f
/g/	got	g
/h/	hot	h
/j/	job	j
/k/	kid	k
/l/	log	l
/m/	man	m
/n/	not	n
/p/	pig	p
/r/	red	r
/s/	sat	s
/t/	top	t
/v/	van	v
/w/	win	w
/z/	zip	z
/ch/	chin	ch
/ng/	sing	ng
/sh/	shop	sh
/th/	thin	th
/th/	then	th
/ks/	tax	x
/kw/	quit	qu

	VOWELS	
SOUND	AS IN	SPELLING
/a/	had	a
/e/	bed	e
/i/	hit	i
/o/	dog	o
/aw/	law	aw
/u/	but	u
/ae/	made	a-e
/ee/	see	ee
/ie/	time	i-e
/oe/	home	o-e
/ue/	cute	u-e
/o͝o/	look	oo
/o͞o/	soon	oo
/ou/	out	ou
/oi/	oil	oi
	VOWEL+R	
/ar/	far	ar
/er/	her	er
/or/	for	or
/e/-/er/	bare	are

Vowel + r vowels have a primary vowel sound followed by an /er/ sound. In the first example, /ar/, this is /ah/ + /er/. Yet these vowels count as one vowel sound. There are nine vowel + r vowels. Only four need to be taught specifically, as the remainder are spelled in Basic Code and can be decoded easily. These are /eer/, /ire/, /ure/, /oor/, /our/ as in *deer, hire, cure, poor, our*. Most vowel sounds have multiple spelling alternatives.

Suggestions for Further Reading

ELIOT, LISE. *What's Going On in There?* New York: Bantam Books, 1999.

An expert on the brain reviews current knowledge on brain and behavioral development for sensory and motor functions, language, and intelligence. She describes normal development as well as developmental disorders. This book is written for parents and professionals.

GOLINKOFF, ROBERTA, AND KATHY HIRSH-PASEK. *How Babies Talk.* New York: Dutton, 1999.

Two top researchers in the field describe language development up to age three. This book is packed with information, and provides firsthand accounts and interesting stories about real children. There are also some useful activities for parents. It is written for parents.

GOPNIK, ALISON, ANDREW MELTZOFF, AND PATRICIA KUHL. *Scientists in the Crib.* New York: Morrow, 1999.

Three top researchers on language and cognitive development write about the development of the brain, visual perception, categorizing, social skills, and language in infants to age four. This is a discussion of fascinating studies on a range of topics. It is written for parents.

HART, BETTY, AND TODD R. RISLEY. *Meaningful Differences.* Baltimore, Md.: Paul H. Brookes, 1995.

A highly readable account of one of the most fascinating studies in the literature on how parents impact the development of their children's language skills. Covers the age range nine months to three years.

McGUINNESS, DIANE. *Why Our Children Can't Read.* New York: Simon and Schuster, 1997.

A thorough analysis of why it has been so hard to teach reading in English-speaking countries, plus information from modern research on what to do about it. Both clinical and classroom methods and approaches are discussed in detail. This book is written for parents and teachers.

McGUINNESS, DIANE. *Early Reading Instruction.* Cambridge, Mass.: MIT Press, in press.

A review of the scientific evidence on writing systems and reading instruction. Topics include the historical data on writing systems, attempts to classify the English spelling system, and a detailed analysis of the research on modern instructional methods for reading, phoneme-awareness training, fluency, vocabulary, and comprehension. Research on spelling is also discussed. The book is suitable for educators, researchers, and parents interested in these topics.

Parent Programs for Home Use with Beginning Readers: Ages Four to Six

LLOYD, SUE. *The Phonics Handbook*. Essex, England: Jolly Learning Ltd., 1998.

This program was designed for the classroom, but can be used by parents. There are brief, easy-to-understand instructions and a training video. The reader is introduced to the sequence for each lesson: the sound to be taught, a matching action pattern, the letter for that sound, and handwriting practice. Each lesson provides a story idea to generate a word that begins with the target sound; parents make up the story. Segmenting and blending exercises receive special attention. There is an emphasis on linking reading and spelling. Spelling dictation is a feature of the lessons. Charts are provided for Basic Code spellings and twenty-two spelling alternatives for vowels. The bulk of the handbook consists of pages of materials (letters and words) that the parent cuts out and uses in the lessons.

Strengths. Lloyd's intimate understanding of how four- and five-year-olds learn is a bonus. Sequence and economy are central to the program. Teaching reading is straightforward and goes quickly. Lessons cover all the necessary elements, plus some spelling alternatives. The program has produced large reading and spelling gains in the classroom in well-conducted research in the classroom in the United Kingdom and Canada, which have been proven to hold up over time.

Weaknesses. Lessons teach isolated words only. No reading materials (poems, stories) are included in the program. Lloyd advises parents to supplement lessons with phonics readers. Multisyllable words are not taught. Only a small portion of spelling alternatives is taught.

McGUINNESS, DIANE. *Sound Steps to Reading.* Forthcoming.

This program was designed specifically for home use for children ages four to six years. It is unique for including all the materials parents will need to teach their child to read, spell, and write. The program contains a brief introduction to orient parents to the program and their role in teaching it. Lessons are self-explanatory and have the same foolproof format throughout. Each lesson begins with a humorous 'parent story,' which features the target sound appearing in all positions in words (first, middle, last), followed by a structured listening exercise in which the child identifies the target sound in all positions in a word. Next, the child sees the letter for that sound, traces it, copies it, and writes it from memory. After three sounds are taught (/p/, /o/, /t/), four words appear made up of the sounds taught so far, with letters segmented on the left, then together on the right. The child says each sound in the word, then blends the sounds into the word. This is followed by spelling dictation for those words. After the first six sounds are taught (lesson 6), short 'readers' appear, consisting of phrases, then sentences and whole stories that use only the sounds and spellings taught so far. The program sequence is determined by the complexity of the spelling code (simple to hard) with spelling gently folded into the lessons so children never become confused. The program teaches the Basic Code plus twenty alternative spellings for consonants and forty-two spellings for vowels. Multisyllable words enter the lessons about halfway through. At the end of the program (fifty to sixty hours), children will be able to read all the parent stories, and will have reading skills at approximately the eight-year-old level or higher.

Strengths. All essential components for reading instruction are contained in the program. Lessons are simple and highly structured. Anyone can teach them. Content is cumulative, with each lesson building on the one before (no sudden jumps or surprises). Spelling is taught in each lesson and directly tied to reading. All main spelling alternatives are included. In field tests, the children and their parents thoroughly enjoyed the parent stories and found the program effective and easy to use.

Weaknesses. Unknown; this is a new program.

See also:

MCGUINNESS, DIANE. *Why Our Children Can't Read.* New York: Simon & Schuster, 1997.

Chapter 9 contains charts and word lists to teach reading basics correctly.

MᶜGUINNESS, DIANE. *Allographs Spelling Program I.* Sea Gate Press. P.O. Box 653, Sanibel, FL 33957.

Contains stories, workbook, dictionary for teaching reading and spelling of common words.

Classroom Programs

LLOYD, SUE. *Jolly Phonics*. Essex, England: Jolly Learning Ltd., 1998.

There is no better program for beginning reading instruction in the classroom available today. This program consistently produces gains of one to two years above control groups and above national norms on standardized reading and spelling tests, and all within about twelve weeks of instruction. There is now a number of quality research studies on this program, and all meet with the same success.

McCRACKEN, G., AND C. C. WALCUTT. *Basic Reading*. Philadelphia, Pa.: Lippincott, 1963.

This program consistently produces gains in the range of six months to a year compared to a contrasting program. This program was tested on five hundred children in 1967 with outstanding results. The efficacy of this program has held up in subsequent research. It appears to have no negative elements or missing elements. It is hard to find, but some versions are available on Amazon.com.

Open Court Reading Grades 1–6. Orlando, Fla.: SRA-McGraw-Hill Publishing (2002).

The main approach and format are in line with the successful programs listed here, but, so far, research on this program is not of a high standard. Gains of about six months on decoding (but not anything else) have been shown in one published study, but only the poorest readers were tested. One questionable element is the use of color-coded backgrounds for consonants and three kinds of vowels. This is confusing (and unnecessary), and can cause difficulties when children transfer to normal text. Also problematic is the practice of intermingling Big Book/read-along activities (whole language) with lessons on learning the code.

This program is hard to get hold of, and teachers must go through the publisher for information, and provide verification of school affiliation.

McGUINNESS, DIANE. *Sound Steps to Reading.* A classroom version of this parent program is in preparation.

For a thorough analysis of these and other programs, see McGuinness, *Early Reading Instruction.*

Remedial Programs for
Clinic and Home Use

McGUINNESS, CARMEN, AND GEOFFREY McGUINNESS. *Reading Reflex*. New York: Simon and Schuster, 1998.

This book presents *Phono-Graphix*, a program originally designed for remediating poor readers in the clinic (with trained tutors). It has been modified for parents. I would not recommend it for children younger than age six. It moves too quickly and assumes prior knowledge, such as knowing letter shapes and how to write them. All consonants and five vowels are taught in Basic Code, and then the logic is switched to multiple spellings for the remaining vowels. This works well for older readers, but not for beginners.

Lessons consist largely of sorting word cards into spelling alternatives for the same sound, or under different decodings of the same letter(s) (to, most, hot). The materials are printed at the back of the book for parents to cut out. There are a few stories for children to read. Includes an exercise called "scratch sheet spelling" in which children are asked to write out all possible spellings of a word they can't spell, then cross off the misspelled words.

Strengths. *Reading Reflex* has a good introduction for the parent. The program is particularly useful for poor readers ages six and up. It has excellent error-correction techniques to break bad habits, and exercises for improving segmenting and blending skills. Tests are provided for the parent to see how the child is progressing. It moves quickly, so children see immediate progress, which increases motivation. Very large gains have been reported in published research on the clinical version of the program (children taught by trained tutors with special materials).

Weaknesses. The progam needs to be supplemented by phonics readers. The "scratch sheet spelling" technique has been discredited in several published studies. These show that looking at misspelled words *increases* spelling errors over the short and long terms, because people become confused about which spelling is correct. (The visual system of the brain automatically codes *what it sees*. It doesn't adjudicate between 'right' and 'wrong.') The sudden shift from a Basic Code to multiple spellings halfway through the lessons is confusing to younger children.

McGUINNESS, DIANE. *Allographs I and II*. Sea Gate Press. P.O. Box 653, Sanibel, FL 33957.

Complete method for teaching the advanced spelling code (multiple spellings for phonemes) which tends to be the main problem for poor readers. Because what you can spell, you can automatically read, this means that *Allographs* boosts both reading and spelling test scores. Students of all ages gain one year or more in 12–20 hours of tutoring. Teaches the entire code including Latin and Greek spelling patterns using a corpus of over 6,000 words.

Strengths: Includes spelling dictionary, workbooks, and readers—all necessary materials. Scripted lessons.

Endnotes

Sources of the quotes used in this book are as follows:

Applebee, A. N. *The Child's Concept of Story*. Chicago: University of Chicago Press, 1978.

Callanan, M. A., and L. M. Oakes. "Preschoolers' Questions and Parents' Explanations: Causal Thinking in Everyday Activity." *Cognitive Development* 7 (1992): 213–233.

Hudson, J. A., and L. R. Shapiro. "From Knowing to Telling: The Development of Children's Scripts, Stories, and Personal Narratives." In *Developing Narrative Structure*, edited by A. McCabe and C. Peterson. Mahwah, N.J.: Lawrence Erlbaum Associates, 1991.

McCabe, A., and C. Peterson. "Getting the Story: A Longitudinal Study of Parental Styles in Eliciting Narratives and Developing Narrative Skill." In *Developing Narrative Structure*, edited by A. McCabe and C. Peterson. Mahwah, N.J.: Lawrence Erlbaum Associates, 1991.

Nelson, K. *Language in Cognitive Development*. Cambridge, England: Cambridge University Press, 1998.

Pinker, S. *The Language Instinct*. New York: William Morrow and Company, 1994.

Index